DON'T BLAME YOUR F#CK UP

ON THE CONSULTANT!

HOW TO BE A BETTER CONSULTING CLIENT AND GET POSITIVE RESULTS

CURTIS L. ODOM, ED.D.

SOPHIA BARRETT, MBA

DON'T BLAME YOUR F#CK UP ON THE CONSULTANT!
HOW TO BE A BETTER CONSULTING CLIENT AND GET POSITIVE RESULTS

CURTIS L. ODOM, ED.D.
SOPHIA BARRETT, MBA

ISBN 978-1-962729-08-6

PUBLISHED BY BOOKNOLOGY (A BUSINESS, CAREER & EDUCATIONAL IMPRINT FROM ADDUCENT)

BOOK•NOL•O•GY
n. delivering useable information and knowledge
that adds value to people's lives

WWW.ADDUCENTCREATIVE.COM
JACKSONVILLE, FLORIDA, USA
PUBLISHED IN THE UNITED STATES OF AMERICA

CONTENTS

DEDICATION

To Brendan Bannister,

Thank you for seeing my potential as an educator before I could see it in myself, for allowing me room to grow and excel, for your mentoring, and for believing in the business professor I could become.

Your guidance to "take the MGMT4501 class content and make it your own" has brought purpose and excitement to my academic career.

For these priceless gifts, I will be forever grateful.

With deep appreciation,

Curtis

ACKNOWLEDGMENTS

To my amazing wife and best friend for life, Nelia, I will never forget that there is no me without you. This seventh book adds yet another chapter to our incredible story. Your willingness to always listen to me talk out my ideas and aspirations as my thinking partner continues to be a blessing. I cannot imagine my life without you sharing every moment with me. Thank you for your undying support. I love you!

To my lovely daughter and best giggle buddy, Alyssa, I've watched you grow from an adorable little girl into a charming young woman. It is a blessing and a privilege to be your father. Daily, I aspire to be your hero and role model for living a grateful life. The greatest joys of my life have been spent sitting next to you on a beach at sunset. I love you!

Curtis L. Odom, Ed.D.

First and foremost, I want to express my deepest gratitude to my partner, Kay. Your unwavering support, patience, and belief in me during this process have been extraordinary. You've been my rock, sounding board, and a constant source of encouragement, and I am eternally grateful for that.

To my parents, thank you for instilling in me the belief that if I put my mind to something, I can accomplish anything. Your love and support have shaped the person I am today, and this book reflects your teachings as it is my own hard work.

And to my dear friends Jane and Jarrod, thank you for always lifting me up with your wisdom and humor and reminding me that no dream is too big if I'm willing to work for it. Your friendship has been an invaluable gift throughout this process.

This book would not have been possible without each of you. Thank you from the bottom of my heart.

Sophia Barrett, MBA

FOREWORD

Within ten years, 2014 to 2024, my organization, Old West Church, went from being a church in debilitating debt to a fiscally and culturally flourishing organization that has since merged with Union Church, creating Union Combined Parish.

In 2018, I sought consultative help. I understood that starting small is essential to growing sustainably and was comfortable with the fact that healthy business growth would take time. I paced myself and knew not to outdo what Old West Church could handle.

First and foremost, I had to believe in what Old West Church could be, and I needed to bring that belief, mindset, and values to the consultant. Old West Church was grossly in debt because of prior management. I recognized that the church's original mission was no longer sustainable and that a change needed to be made as expediently as possible. We had over five million dollars' worth of renovations and repairs that needed to happen to protect the building. There were 30 congregation members, most at or below the poverty line and all at different life stages. I knew this needed to change, as the church could not sustain itself from the donations the congregation could contribute. I also believed in the change but didn't know how it could happen.

And that is why I reached out for consultative help. By June of 2023, I helped oversee the merger and acquisition of two other churches. We now have $45 million worth of assets. Yes, Old West Church went from $3 million to $45 million in a year.

During my first interaction with the consultants, they asked me what I needed to fix and what direction I had for them. Instead of trying to maintain control over the situation, I declared that I would be a part of the process and work with the consultants rather than tell them what to do. I decided not to be the standard-bearer for the organization, as I needed change, not more of the same. I spent much of my time learning who the consultants were, their values, interests, talents, and more. I viewed the consultants holistically and analyzed how to equip those traits to leverage them for where the project could go.

Throughout my interactions with the consultants, I felt motivated by others' creativity instead of feeling negatively when a suggestion was shared that I had not thought of. The more creative ideas they shared, the more I started feeling like a seismic shift for the organization was possible but would be larger and more innovative than I could have imagined. I made sure never to discount an idea right off the bat. I even encouraged the consultants that their consultative relationship with me allowed them to try something bold. I wanted to create an opportunity for the consultants to learn in a safe space, just like I was learning from them. And that is how the church became focused on food justice and fighting racial inequality.

While it may be easy to think this could only have happened with consultative help, this may be true. However, consultative help was necessary, but more was needed for this success. I had to take a leap of faith, as Old West Church was a non-profit, and many consultants tend to avoid non-profit consultancy. Nevertheless, I advocated for myself and the organization. My attitude and commitment to the entire consultative process led to the significant success of Old West Church. I went into every consultative engagement with a healthy mindset, in the spirit of support, curiosity, wonder, and an intentional lack of defensiveness.

I had a solid basis for my values, as well as the values of Old West Church, and I made sure that they stayed consistent and complemented each other. I entered every interaction with an empathic lens, doing my best to see each decision and suggestion the consultants made through their eyes. I communicated consistently with the consultants by actively listening and discussing my doubts to create trust. I was honest, both with my expectations and satisfaction toward the consultants, but also with myself. I made sure her enthusiasm for the process was palpable. I was grateful for the help and kept myself motivated throughout the process. I ensured that I was entirely physically and mentally present for the consultants, as I knew my disengaging would only risk the project's ultimate success.

Lastly, I wanted these changes to be implemented in the organization. I was willing to continue adapting to the ever-changing consultative environment and growing with the project, which led to Old West Church's success. It is also essential to add that Old West Church's exponential growth resulted from a series of consultative relationships over several years.

In a good way, this was a seismic shift. By working with consultants and committing myself to the process, I was able to successfully cultivate lasting change and set myself up for future change to be just as successful. I will continue pushing for food justice and fighting racial inequality, such as creating affordable and ADA-compliant housing and a food forest in the front yard of the building. I aim for this space to be a place for all people, regardless of identity, to be fed and housed.

With a recent goal to focus on food justice accomplished, we have transformed the front yard into a food forest with raised beds, fruit trees, a living wall, and a pollinator garden. While no one knows where things could go from year to year, the sky is truly the limit! This is an example of starting small and growing sustainably.

This successful consultative business relationship example teaches that collaboration and consistency surrounding all facets of a consultative client relationship can create significant positive change. All team members must be willing to keep an open mind, as just because someone is different from you in some way or that they had an idea you did not think of does not mean that the concept is any less valuable.

The most impactful changes can result from a suggestion that you have never considered before, which is why consultants are often hired—to think outside the box. Old West Church benefited from the willingness of the entire leadership team to be the best consulting clients we could be and achieve positive results for the church and the community.

As a reader, I wish you well on your journey to getting positive results while becoming a better consulting client.

Rev. Dr. Sara Garrard
Executive Pastor
Union Combined Parish
https://www.unionboston.org/pastor/sara

PREFACE

A lot of positive change can happen in a short amount of time when everyone's values and expectations are aligned. Ideally, the consultant and the client should align in a consultative business relationship. The media and popular books always emphasize how to be a good consultant, a successful consultant, and how to become a consultant. Yet, there is minimal, if not no, emphasis on what it means to be a good consulting client.

A positive relationship requires equal effort from all parties involved, but there needs to be more guidance on how to flourish as a client in a consultative relationship. Even when clients are the focus, that focus is primarily on why they aren't as effective as they should be—it has to do with dissatisfaction. Therefore, this book will highlight how to be a better consulting client.

Before we go too far, let's address the elephant in the room: the title of our book, *Don't Blame Your F#ck Up On The Consultant*.

The short answer is that we wanted a provocative title to grab your attention and convey our book's central message boldly and unapologetically. The title's adult humor aims to connect with you as a reader who has firsthand experience with poor consulting engagement results, making the book both relatable and genuine. Our book addresses criticisms and misconceptions about consultants, primarily that they serve as mere scapegoats for broader organizational failures.

We recognized that a blunt title would help the book stand out in a crowded market, especially in genres like self-help, business, and career. Our choice of title signals that we intend to be direct, straightforward, and unconventional. We aimed to elicit an immediate reaction by crafting a memorable and intriguing title. Our title is intentional and fits with the book's edgy style, reflecting current societal trends and the casual evolution of language in public discourse.

We wanted to be bold, irreverent, and authentic. We believed that using profanity in our title would pique your curiosity enough to inspire you to pick up this book and start reading.

Were we wrong?

In this book, we discuss how to be the kind of client consultants dream of working with. We also explore what makes a better consulting client or even a good prospective client for those who have yet to work with a consultant. This flips the script. We often talk about finding the right consultant to hire, but what about being the right client? What we share in this book goes well beyond that. It's all about understanding the dynamics of a true partnership and how to get the best from any collaboration.

This book lays it all out by presenting ten key qualities, which we call coins, for a truly successful consulting relationship. What we find most interesting is that these **10 coins** are universal currency for any collaboration. Think about it—office teamwork, playing on a sports team, those tricky group projects, even family matters. As you read, the book opens with the incredible story of Old West Church. They were drowning in debt, but within a few years, they became a thriving organization with $45,000,000 in assets. It all began with their approach to consulting. It's a remarkable turnaround story highlighting the power of the right mindset. The church leader, Reverend Dr. Sarah Garrard, understood that growth takes time. Starting small was crucial, but most importantly, she viewed the consultants she worked with as genuine partners, not just people hired to come in, fix things, and leave.

This brings us to the **1st coin—Mindset**. Mindset is not just about wanting help; it's about being genuinely open to receiving help—this is a different ballgame. It reminded us of the concept of a fixed mindset versus a growth mindset. If you come in with a fixed mindset—believing, "I've got this; I know everything"—you will need to be more receptive to new ideas. You must adopt a growth mindset, which is fundamental to being a great client. It's about being open to new possibilities, challenging our assumptions, and focusing, where it should be, on results rather than our ego. Reverend Dr. Garrard exemplified this. She was not only open to ideas but energized by them. That kind of openness becomes contagious, setting a positive tone for the collaborative process.

Setting that tone is the **2nd coin—Values**. More than simply having your mission statement on the wall is needed. You must understand what your organization stands for and how those values manifest. You must also articulate those values to your consultant to ensure their recommendations align with what you genuinely believe. Otherwise, you'll end up with solutions that might look good on paper but don't resonate with your organization's DNA.

Creating that match is the **3rd coin—Empathy**. Although commonly associated with personal relationships, empathy is equally vital in business. This is a common misconception. Think about it:

you're hiring a consultant to help you improve, right? Improvement often involves confronting hard truths about what isn't working. It's about accepting constructive feedback without becoming defensive or shutting down. You have to recognize that the consultant isn't personally attacking you; they're trying to help you achieve your goals, even if that means delivering news you might not want to hear.

Recently, we witnessed someone receive some harsh feedback. We are sure their first instinct was to become defensive, but they took a moment to pause and then used the empathy coin. It seemed as if they tried to listen and understand the other person's perspective. It made the whole experience much less painful, and we learned a lot from it. This is an excellent example of how these principles can apply outside a formal consulting relationship. That initial defensiveness is a natural reaction, but by consciously choosing empathy, you create a space for real growth and accurate understanding. Sometimes, being open to seeing things from another's perspective can be challenging. It takes practice. However, the book includes some excellent real-world examples of the power of empathy, even in business. We share a story about a retail company that responded to the COVID-19 pandemic with extraordinary empathy for their employees and customers. You know what? They saw increased loyalty and even better results because of it. This story demonstrates that empathy isn't just a touchy-feely concept; it can impact a company's success.

What makes the difference is the **4th coin—Listening**. Listening goes beyond merely hearing what the consultant has to say. There's an art to effective listening, especially in a collaborative setting. It involves active engagement, asking clarifying questions, and striving to understand the nuances of what the consultant is communicating. The book introduces a framework for active listening that we hope you'll find helpful. This framework is based on four key questions to ask yourself while listening. First, what did I learn from this? Second, what surprised me? Third, what resonated with me? And finally, the most crucial question: What action will I take based on what I've heard?

This framework shifts you from passive listening to processing and applying the information. It reminds us of the practice of reflecting on conversations afterward to ensure we absorbed everything and know our next steps. It demonstrates a genuine commitment to maximizing the collaboration.

Speaking of maximizing our efforts, let's discuss the **5th coin—Communication**. This concept may seem straightforward, but there's much more to it than simply talking to your consultant. Effective communication encompasses much more than mere words. It requires clarity, consistency, and a real focus on ensuring everyone is on the same page while being transparent about their needs and expectations. It is also connected to self-awareness. Understanding style, strengths, and weaknesses can make a significant difference, as can recognizing potential blind spots in your communication. That awareness is essential for communicating as clearly and compellingly as possible.

This brings us to a closely related **6th coin—Trust. Trust** isn't a given. You should be able to trust the consultant you're working with. While trust is essential, the book presents a thought-provoking perspective on it. Rather than waiting for the consultant to earn your trust, begin by giving them the benefit of the doubt. Trust their expertise until there's a reason not to. It's almost like flipping the script on the whole trust concept. It makes me think of the saying, 'Assume positive intent.' If you approach the relationship believing the consultant is genuinely there to help you, it creates a different dynamic. That initial trust fosters a much more open and collaborative relationship. You're more likely to be honest about your challenges, more receptive to new ideas, and ultimately gain more value from the engagement.

Speaking of honesty, which brings us to the **7th coin—Honesty**. Honesty and trust are two sides of the same coin, and they go hand in hand. Like trust, the book emphasizes a proactive approach to honesty.

This involves being transparent about your organization's challenges right from the start, including the issues that may be embarrassing or uncomfortable to acknowledge. It's about recognizing that vulnerability can be a strength, particularly in a collaborative environment. The book illustrates this with an analogy about getting to Las Vegas. Imagine you're the client telling the consultant you want to reach Vegas, but you forget to mention that you're already in Nevada and know the way there. This isn't about intentionally misleading the consultant; it's more about a lack of self-awareness and honesty regarding your starting point. The most successful clients are brutally honest about their situation, even if it's painful. It's like ripping off a Band-Aid—it might sting at first, but afterward, you can start to heal and move forward. That honesty enables the consultant to create a relevant and effective plan, saving time and resources while preventing later frustration.

The way to combat frustration is with the **8th coin: Enthusiasm**. It's more than just showing up with a smile; genuine enthusiasm has real power for both the client and the consultant. When the client is genuinely excited about the process and the potential for positive change, it generates contagious positive energy. As a result, everyone works at their best.

This shared enthusiasm fosters a more collaborative and, ultimately, more successful engagement. Everyone's rowing in the same direction with greater energy and purpose. You're all in the same boat, paddling toward the same destination. The book also emphasizes the downside of this; when a client lacks enthusiasm, it can weigh a project down. Yes, it's like having a lead weight in the boat. While everyone is working harder, the ship just isn't moving. It's demoralizing and causes everyone to question whether the effort is worth it.

This brings us to the **9th coin**—Presence. This requirement extends beyond just being physically present. It involves being fully engaged, both emotionally and mentally. Give your complete attention and participate in the process meaningfully. It's about being fully committed, not just occupying space in the room. I recognize how this can significantly enhance the quality of collaboration. Consider it this way: when a client is genuinely present, it demonstrates respect for the consultant's time and expertise and the project's significance. In this regard, it fosters a much more productive and collaborative environment. Indeed, you're communicating, "I value your time, I appreciate your input, and I'm here to engage with you on this." This contrasts sharply with checking your phone during meetings or zoning out while the consultant speaks. Such distractions signal a lack of investment, which can be incredibly frustrating for a consultant.

Finally, we present you with the **10th coin— Willingness**. What does it mean to be a willing client? Willingness involves recognizing that consulting is not a passive process. It's not merely about hiring someone to come in and wave a magic wand to fix all your problems. It requires effort, commitment, and the readiness to step outside your comfort zone. It's about being prepared to roll up your sleeves and do the work. Exactly. It's also about being open to adapting to your expectations.

The consultant might suggest a solution completely different from what you had in mind, or they may challenge you to view things from a new perspective. This goes back to the idea of having a growth mindset. Being open to new possibilities and letting go of preconceived notions is essential. Absolutely.

It also connects to trust: If you trust your consultant's expertise, you're more likely to be receptive to their suggestions, even if they're unexpected.

You say, "Okay, I trust you to guide me on this journey, even if it takes me down an unexpected path." This is about surrendering to the process and embracing the unknown.

These **10 coins** represent currency for building a successful consulting relationship, but they can be applied to more than just hiring a consultant. You can use these coins to become a better partner, leader, and, ultimately, a more effective and fulfilled individual.

WHY HIRE A CONSULTANT

What prompts someone to hire a consultant? No matter whom you ask, you might receive a different answer to that question each time. If there isn't a straightforward answer, what are the processes, expectations, and lessons to follow to hire the best consultant for each challenge? Regardless of that response, the necessity of hiring a consultant comes down to the need for someone outside an organization to enter that organization and help resolve a problem that those within the organization could not, don't wish to, or believe is better addressed by someone else.

Consulting involves an organization having a vision of where it wants to go, perhaps understanding its starting point, but then needing assistance to identify the gap or the distance between its desired destination and current position. Therefore, it requires an advisor or partner to help navigate that gap between the desired future and present state. While this may seem simplistic to describe consulting, facilitating the journey from where you are to where you want to be, it genuinely captures the essence of consulting.

However, the critical factor for anyone considering hiring a consultant is their willingness to consider other perspectives and view their business through different lenses.

Ultimately, it's about being open to accepting the help offered. Furthermore, consultants do not do the work which appeals to many people. Some aspire to be consultants because they believe consultants spend all day generating ideas while others handle the work, leading to a favorable outcome for everyone. Unfortunately, this is a misconception. To be a consultant, one must be an expert in a specific area.

Being an expert is a title you can't give yourself unless you want to be seen as pompous or viewed as a jackass by others. An expert is a title awarded by others. So, how do you achieve that expert status? By producing results through consistent actions that lead to measurable outcomes and helping others succeed. If we understand why we hire a consultant, shouldn't we first assess whether we're ready to be a client? This is where things start to get exciting. It begins with recognizing the need for assistance within the company, realizing that what you've done hasn't necessarily worked or that some efforts have succeeded. Still, now you need to pivot or ramp up for greater speed.

Knowing you need help doesn't always mean you're ready to work with a consultant. It doesn't imply you're prepared to be a client, but that's the situation we find ourselves in. This idea is the foundation of the book you are about to read. For instance, involving an expert or consultant might make you feel it reflects on your capabilities in your field. In truth, it has nothing to do with your skills. This crucial distinction deserves emphasis. Additionally, individuals who link their self-worth to their achievements may struggle to recognize this.

You might need more time to be ready to hire a consultant for various reasons. Hiring the wrong consultant, or perhaps the individual, business, or organization, while needing consulting requires more time to become a better client. In this book, we'll discuss common themes that explain why some organizations have succeeded after seeking consulting. We'll also look at organizations that have yet to achieve successful consulting outcomes. We won't mention specific names, as that is unimportant. Instead, we will examine how utilizing the **10 coins** has enabled organizations to thrive and foster meaningful interactions between the consultant and the organization receiving the consulting.

Additionally, we'll reflect on takeaways and themes that have led to challenging and detrimental interactions between an organization and its hired consultants. In other words, we will explore what it looks like when you're in the right mindset and location to be consulted and what occurs when you're at the wrong time or in the wrong place for consultation. This will make this book somewhat different from what you might have read before or expect.

When we began considering the book, we conducted research, and as you might expect, we surveyed the landscape and discovered many books discussing what it's like to be a consultant. What is it like to hire a consultant? We encountered numerous ideas about what constitutes a poor consultant. We came across ample writings on what happens when consulting goes awry. However, what we did not find—and why this book will contribute to the conversation—is any books, writings, assessments, or articles that address how to be a good _**client**_.

How do you become, be, and remain a good consulting client? As much as it depends on the consultant providing the "expert advice" to guide you from your current state to your desired future state—closing that gap between the two—it also hinges on the consultant's proficiency in client interactions, achieving reasonable client satisfaction, maintaining a good reputation, having a strong brand, and more. What about the internal checklist you or your organization should address first to ensure that you ask, "Are we ready to think differently about our organization? Are we prepared to move in a different direction or at a different pace?" It all boils down to this intriguing little component.

There's a difference between wanting consulting help and being willing to be a consulting client. You still have to be convinced, even if you have wished for consulting assistance.

In the consulting engagement, you may need to think, act, speak, and behave differently as a business owner or senior leader than you have in the past. This willingness comes from your desire to achieve the results you are pursuing. It involves being open to critically evaluating yourself or your organization and acknowledging, "You know what, perhaps we need to approach things differently if we want to succeed." Are you prepared to heed the expertise you are hiring or bringing into the organization?

This essential checklist will form the basis of what you'll read in this book. It begins with self-awareness among a company's senior leaders and their willingness to engage as consulting clients. We hope this book proves helpful to you and serves as a starting point for developing the mindset necessary to determine if you truly want to enter a consultative relationship.

There is no shame in starting a consulting engagement and realizing that it may not be right for you, us, or your organization. The harm arises from continuing an engagement without assessing whether you are ready, whether your business is prepared, and whether you are willing to implement any recommendations or suggestions the consulting firm or consultant offers to effect change.

The consultants can provide a plan, including an implementation plan, detailing what you should do, how to do it, and when. However, following the recommendations rests solely with the business, its leaders, and its employees.

Some people want success and results, yet they are unwilling to put in the necessary work to achieve them. It's important to communicate this upfront rather than reveal it at the end of a consulting engagement where there's a chance of spending large sums of money for expertise.

Bringing in knowledge without taking action is not an investment; it's merely an expense. When you seek consultative help, you gain new perspectives that can propel the organization, the leaders, or you—reading this book—forward with practical steps toward that desired future state, becoming an effective consulting client.

As we contemplated writing this book, we considered the best way to structure it. We wanted the book to be concise and offer more than a quick read that leaves you wondering, "Why did I spend my money on this?" As mentioned earlier, we decided to reflect on various behaviors and key takeaways from years of research focusing on opposites. What actions have clients taken that led to their success? We showcase examples of consulting clients at both ends of the spectrum. Then, we share insights and themes from what clients have done that either helped or hindered them in achieving their desired results from working with a consultant. We planned to assemble a set of chapters, ten in total, that examine these contrasting approaches.

We also decided to explore the flip side of the **10 coins** mentioned earlier, in no particular order. These important coins include mindset, values, empathy, listening, communication, trust, honesty, enthusiasm, presence, and willingness.

We invite you to consider these **10 coins** and how they appear at both ends of the spectrum. By the time you finish reading this book, you will understand how to be a good consulting client and, perhaps more importantly, how to conduct some self-assessment to determine if you're ready for the consulting you claim to want. Are you prepared to embark on this journey? Are you willing and able to listen, communicate, and demonstrate trust and honesty?

Can you be present with everything happening in the business? Do you understand your values? What is your mindset right now? We hope to provide you with all of these insights within the scope of this book to assist you in understanding what it looks like. Ask yourself, "Am I ready for these takeaways or behaviors, or am I just paying lip service to them?" Answer honestly, or you risk having your organization spend money it shouldn't.

What are we saying? Being a better consulting client starts with how you show up, thinking about what you'll engage in, and whether you are ready to be a client. We hope this book helps you determine where you are, where you're going, and what it will take to close the gap between those two places.

Mindset

In consulting, mindset—the collection of attitudes, beliefs, and thought processes that a client brings to an engagement—plays a crucial role in determining the success or failure of the consulting relationship. A client's mindset can influence a project's tone, direction, and impact. This chapter examines what constitutes a strong mindset in a consultative relationship, addresses the challenges of a weak mindset, and offers real-world examples illustrating both. By understanding how mindset affects consulting outcomes, organizations can better prepare to maximize consulting relationships to their full potential.

One should adopt a particular mindset before entering consulting. In this case, we refer to mindset to inquire whether the organization's leadership possesses expertise and passion for its mission.

In other words, do the organization's leaders loom large or small? Do they possess a passion for the organization's mission and vision? What have you accomplished? Are they engaged with it? Do they feel it's their responsibility to help the organization achieve its vision and mission? Were they present during the early stages of the organization? Did they assist in crafting the vision statement? Were they involved in its inception?

Based on three years of research and almost a hundred interviews, to have the right mindset for consulting and being a good client, you need to approach this with a personal interest in seeing the organization succeed. You should feel connected and committed to the organization's vision and mission and want to leave it better than you found it. You want the organization to grow rather than stagnate and transition from its current state to the desired future.

It's going to take a lot of work. We may need to invest time, energy, and money in reaching our goals, which aligns with the idea that becoming someone you've never been before requires doing things you've never done. For some, that can be a daunting prospect. It's frightening to recognize that by expressing a desire to work with a consultant, you acknowledge that some change is necessary. However, being aware that change is needed is not the same as being fully committed to the change that must occur. Hiring a consultant presents an exciting opportunity because it shows you understand you can't do it alone. It acknowledges that you haven't succeeded, but you genuinely want to change and accept your need for assistance.

Help may be needed for various reasons, including expansion, growth, cost savings, business streamlining, mergers, and acquisitions. It depends on what your organization requires to achieve its vision and mission. If the leadership had that expertise, they wouldn't need a consultant; however, the leadership often requires assistance or validation. Numerous organizations have hired consultants not because they lacked knowledge but because they sought validation for their actions. They desired an external 'expert' to affirm for internal leadership, the board of directors, or others that what the organization has been doing is the right course.

Thus, the right mindset is essential for approaching the consulting engagement with a clear end goal. As we mentioned, the opposite mindset involves being inflexible, having a singular solution in mind, and resisting your consultant's alternative or more creative suggestions.

There are many instances when the organization or individual seeking consulting only wants to hear themselves speak. In other words, they want to focus on the validation aspect, as we mentioned. There is nothing wrong with wanting validation, but what happens when you seek it as a consulting client? When working with a consultant, you and the consultant may realize there is a better way to approach the tasks. The objective perspective and the consultant's outside view can identify aspects you haven't noticed. They can point out things you should have recognized. They perceive details in ways you may have overlooked due to your long and intense involvement with the organization. When they present these insights, are you open to accepting them? Or is your mindset so rigid that you take this new, potentially more creative suggestion personally, perceiving it as a critique or an attack on everything that has occurred, whether it was your contributions or those made by others in the organization?

Of course, we're sure you know that the consultant is not attacking you. We're confident you understand that having an outside set of eyes— one consultant, multiple consultants, or even a team—is precisely what you hired them for. You've brought them in to assess the current situation, reflect on past events, and consider future steps. In consulting terms, that's known as intake and due diligence. You are attempting to grasp where the organization stands, where it has been, and how it arrived at this point. So, once you have a clear understanding of the business's origin story and the reasons behind this need, you can begin to explore how you can align the perspectives of the consulting group with those of the stakeholders who engaged our consultative assistance.

If we're in a situation where the client's mindset is crucial—this also ties into how one becomes an excellent client—don't hire a consultant if your mindset is more closed than open. If you're unwilling to think differently, have someone challenge your existing thoughts and actions, or consider that a new approach might be better, reconsider. Don't engage a consultant if you're not ready to set aside your ego and emotions. If you can't do this, you're already on the path to not being a good consulting client.

Consultants prefer working with organizations that have an open or growth mindset. They look for organizations that recognize their current state but can also envision their future. Their mindset focuses on who they can become, what they can accomplish, and what they can achieve. Speaking as a consultant once more, that forward-looking mindset is the type of organization we enjoy collaborating with, especially leaders dedicated to success and results. They employ a success-oriented mindset and do not take it personally when a consultant suggests that what was cannot stay the same if you wish to reach what will be; this is a crucial concept.

So, mindset, where is your mindset? What must you do to prepare your mind for this type of work? Examine your organization, the leadership team, and yourself. Is it possible that you've been viewing this situation for so long and through the same lenses or mirrors that you can only perceive it in one way? Is your mindset such that you're open to—this relates to a topic we'll discuss later—are you willing to have it changed, to be influenced, or directed toward a new way of thinking that leads to a new way of being?

THE POWER OF A STRONG MINDSET IN CONSULTING RELATIONSHIPS

A strong mindset in consulting is marked by openness, curiosity, and a readiness to participate in collaborative problem-solving. Clients with this mindset are receptive to new ideas, ready to tackle challenges, and view consultants as partners rather than just vendors. They are prepared to examine their assumptions, address organizational issues directly, and take a proactive role in achieving their desired outcomes. Let's consider a client who exemplified these qualities.

Case Example: A Growth Mindset Client

Consider the case of an international retail company encountering significant disruption from online competitors. The company hired a consulting firm to modernize its operations, reimagine the customer experience, and streamline its supply chain. The client's leadership team showed a strong, growth-oriented mindset. Here's how:

1. Openness to New Ideas: The client's executives approached the project without preconceived notions about the solution. Although initially skeptical about integrating advanced AI tools into their operations, they became willing to explore the idea when the consultants demonstrated the benefits. This openness resulted in the discovery of previously untapped opportunities for personalization in their online shopping experience.

2. Curiosity and Active Engagement: Rather than expecting the consultants to deliver solutions in isolation, the client's team actively engaged in problem-solving. They arranged regular brainstorming sessions with the consultants, openly discussing operational challenges and posing questions to understand emerging technologies better. They quickly aligned with the consultants on key objectives by remaining curious and involved.

3. Willingness to Confront Challenges: The client recognized long-standing inefficiencies in their supply chain and faced possible layoffs as part of the modernization effort. Although these were sensitive issues, they approached them transparently by holding open forums with employees to convey the necessity for change.

They collaborated closely with consultants to develop a respectful transition plan, reducing potential employee resistance and ensuring continuity.

This client adeptly navigated the disruptive changes in the retail industry by maintaining a strong mindset. Their openness, curiosity, and courage enabled them to make informed decisions, integrate innovative solutions, and remain competitive.

A weak mindset in consulting can be characterized by rigidity, defensiveness, and an excessive reliance on internal biases. Clients with a weak mindset may regard consultants with suspicion, resist new ideas, and sometimes undermine the consulting engagement by withholding information or sabotaging recommended changes. This defensive stance restricts the consultants' ability to offer practical solutions. It limits the client's perspective, making them less adaptable and less resilient to change.

Case Example: A Fixed Mindset Client

A manufacturing company hired a consulting firm to find ways to enhance their production processes. However, the leadership team maintained a rigid, fixed mindset that significantly restricted the project's effectiveness. Here's what went wrong:

1. Resistance to Change: The client dismissed suggestions involving significant modifications to their current production line. Although the consultants' analysis indicated substantial cost savings through automation, the executives refused to consider altering their manual processes, citing concerns about "maintaining control" and potential union issues. This resistance effectively stunted any discussion of digital transformation.

2. Defensiveness and Lack of Transparency: The client's leadership perceived the consultants' recommendations as criticisms of their established practices. Rather than viewing feedback constructively, they reacted defensively, selectively withholding data highlighting inefficiencies and presenting incomplete metrics to "prove" their methods were adequate. This lack of transparency obstructed the consultants' ability to make informed recommendations and fostered a tense, adversarial atmosphere.

3. Over-reliance on Internal Perspectives: The leadership team believed they understood their processes better than any outsider could, leading them to dismiss external viewpoints. This insular approach prevented them from recognizing best practices that had been successful in other

manufacturing contexts, limiting their ability to learn from broader industry insights.

Ultimately, the project stagnated, and the manufacturing company missed the chance to streamline production and lower costs. The client's fixed mindset transformed the engagement into an expensive endeavor with little impact.

KEY MINDSET ATTRIBUTES

The contrasting examples illustrate that a client's mindset can be an asset or a hindrance to a consulting relationship. Key qualities of a strong and growth-focused mindset include:

1. Openness to New Ideas: Clients open to considering and exploring new perspectives can discover creative solutions and benefit from broader industry insights.
2. Curiosity and Active Engagement: When clients are actively involved in the process, they provide essential context, align more swiftly with consultants, and enhance the likelihood of actionable outcomes.
3. Willingness to Confront Challenges: Clients who recognize the need to tackle deep-rooted issues—even when uncomfortable—can significantly improve their operations.

On the other hand, a weak or fixed mindset in consulting relationships often manifests as:

1. Resistance to Change: Clients often resist adapting, limiting the effectiveness of consulting as they cling to outdated practices or avoid the discomfort of change.

2. Defensiveness and Lack of Transparency: When clients perceive feedback as criticism instead of constructive input, they limit the consultant's capacity to analyze and suggest improvements.

3. Over-reliance on internal perspectives limits openness to external expertise, narrowing the client's vision and restricting opportunities for innovation.

In consulting, mindset plays a key role in success. Clients who approach consulting with a strong, growth-oriented mindset are better equipped to fully leverage the consultants' expertise, insights, and resources, collaborate effectively with the consulting team, embrace new ideas, and face organizational challenges with an openness that fosters positive change. Conversely, a weak, fixed mindset limits opportunities for valuable learning and meaningful progress, often making consulting engagements futile or frustrating experiences.

Fostering a strong mindset and leadership across teams is essential for organizations seeking to maximize the value of their consulting investments. A growth mindset cultivates an environment where consultants and clients can collaborate effectively to achieve significant and lasting improvements.

This collaborative spirit enhances the project's impact and strengthens the organization's resilience and adaptability in a rapidly changing business landscape.

VALUES

Values define the core of any organization. They are guiding principles that shape a company's culture, inform decision-making, and influence its relationships.

Values are especially critical for organizations engaged in consultative relationships. They dictate how clients and consultants approach challenges, make compromises, and ultimately achieve success. This chapter explores the significance of organizational values in a consultative setting, examining the positive impact of adhering to values and the consequences of failing to uphold them.

Values reflect the mission and vision, and if the organization's values are thoughtfully established in advance, do we truly understand what we value as an organization? Are we clear about what we aspire to value? If customer service or focus is a priority, what steps are we taking to ensure that? How does our vision or mission align with these priorities? When people arrive at the organization each day, what motivates them to come to work? Which values resonate most with people regarding the culture and the organization's deliverables or operations?

The question should be asked whether you will become a consulting client. Do you understand the organization's values? Are you aware of the culture? Based on that understanding, can you grasp what will and won't work? Why do we mention this? Because it's easy to assume that hiring a consultant means they will come in and change everything. From our experience as consultants, we can tell you that's a daunting reality. Almost no consultant, and certainly none that we've encountered, claims to be an expert or possesses expertise, to put it better, in every area where you might seek help. They have specific knowledge, skills, and abilities in a few places, but not all, where you may need assistance.

Suppose you consider the values of the organization and its culture. In that case, it's essential that, before hiring a consultant, you can explain these values in a way that others can easily understand, even if they haven't worked in the organization. It's not helpful if the only way to grasp your values is through being a member of the organization. When hiring a consultant, ask yourself if you can clearly articulate your organization's vision, mission, and values so the consultant or consulting group can propose solutions aligned with your foundational values.

The idea is that if a consultant—my favorite, a change agent, usually the title given to someone within the organization—they won't call you a consultant; they'll call you a change agent. However, in reality, you'll be doing some internal consulting.

The key point is that if the consultant or change agent has not considered the organization's vision, mission, and values when crafting a consultative solution, it's likely to fail upon arrival. If you are willing to share, explain, and help someone from the outside understand the organization's values—information they need to get up to speed and succeed—you're ready to be a client.

However, only hire a consultant if you are knowledgeable about these matters. Being well-versed in your organization's vision, mission, and values can lead to realistic expectations of the consultant rather than expecting them to work miracles or disregard the organization's core values. That is a dangerous approach. Suppose you are not a consultant entering an organization, reflecting on past experiences, and determining what suggestions, solutions, and recommendations you can offer to meet the client's needs. In that case, you risk overpromising and setting the stage for under-delivery. If you have unrealistic expectations, you should reconsider being a consulting client. The reason is that you are setting yourself up for disappointment.

When you take the opportunity to understand your desired future state and confront your organization's current state, whatever distance exists between the two, I doubt you'll achieve it with just a wave of a magic wand. Moving from where you are to where you want to be will require time, energy, and resources. Part of realizing that now depends on expectations. What's a realistic expectation of what we will accomplish after hiring a consultant? What will we achieve that is directly related to the consultant's suggestions and recommendations? What can we achieve based on our internal knowledge, skill, and ability to implement those suggestions or recommendations? In other words, can we—grounded in our values, mission, and vision—collaborate with the consultant to create the right-sized solution?

Part of what enables you to be a consulting client is understanding that the consultant will only handle some tasks for you. The consultant is not there to work for your business or you personally but to collaborate 'with' you alongside the company and the leadership team. This means the organization plays an active role in upholding its culture and values while progressing toward becoming the organization you have not been before, as you undertake actions you have not done before.

Now, take a moment to reflect. When you consider your organization's vision, mission, and values, is one or more of these elements hindering your ability to close the gap between your current position and your desired destination?

After hiring consultants, is it easy to hear from the consultant again, who offers their honest opinion from an outside perspective? Are they not trying to blame or suggest that people aren't doing their jobs properly? But what if the organization's vision, mission, and values hinder its success? What happens if the consultant points out unrealistic expectations contradicting the organization's core values? Based on these values, is there a willingness to change direction, seek greater clarity, and then determine how to move forward... or not? These are some things we should be considering. These elements touch on the concept of value. Another aspect of value that deserves discussion is its role in determining who is the most knowledgeable. Is the value related to healthy competition, or is it about results?

We've consulted for and worked with some organizations focusing on achieving results. These organizations are all about making things happen. An organization doesn't need to state this explicitly; every organization has the potential to grow and achieve results. The fundamental idea is that a business's purpose is to remain viable. However, these values are essential.

You can't be an effective consulting client if you don't fully understand your organization's vision, mission, and values or if you can't recognize them when they're actively demonstrated. This also applies if you enter the relationship with unrealistic expectations, which we have witnessed. We've seen organizations hire consultants or consulting groups expecting to relax as if they were on a mini vacation, so to speak.

In contrast, the consultants or consulting group solves all their problems for them without realizing that the work will be done with them rather than for them. Are you an ambassador for the organization's values? Do you understand what the organization values overall? And can you collaborate with a consultant to ensure that what you're bringing on board integrates well once it's there? That's the critical piece. Do our values enable us to reap the benefits of the consulting assistance we will receive? Are we in a place, space, and time where the culture's values are understood, or are we in a transitional period with leadership coming or going? That's the wrong time to engage a consultant because your culture is in flux.

If you believe leaders shape an organization's culture, it makes sense to consider who the leaders are. What are they doing to create, sustain, or grow that culture? And are we prepared to bring someone from outside into that environment?

If the value of the consultant is to help you succeed, and if the consultant is working with you for your success, are you prepared to meet them there? Are you as committed to your results as the consultant you've hired? We hold onto phrases that keep us grounded: I can't want success for my clients more than they want it for themselves. That's a powerful way to think about being a consulting client. What do I value? What am I hoping to gain as a result? And am I able to do my part to make that happen?

WHY VALUES MATTER IN CONSULTING

Values are not merely ideals or lofty aspirations but the foundation for the entire organization. Aligning values can enhance trust, clarify goals, and foster genuine collaboration in a consultative relationship. When both the client and consultant work within a framework of shared values, it encourages open communication, commitment, and the capacity to navigate complex situations effectively.

In consulting, values can guide problem-solving approaches, define ethical boundaries, and influence how an organization manages change and innovation.

They can help organizations resist short-term gains that compromise long-term integrity, drive, or alignment with stakeholder needs. However, merely declaring values isn't sufficient; organizations must demonstrate their commitment by adhering to these principles, especially under pressure.

Strong Example: Values as a Driver of Trust and Success

Consider the case of a global technology company that hired a consultancy to assist with a large-scale transformation initiative. This company had a clear core value highlighting innovation, transparency, and customer-centricity. As the project commenced, the company and the consultancy intentionally ensured these values would shape every aspect of the partnership.

The consulting team presented recommendations during the transformation that disrupted the existing operating model. Rather than responding defensively or reluctantly, the client embraced its value of transparency.

The executive team encouraged employees to participate in updates, openly communicated the reasons for the changes, and welcomed feedback from all levels of the organization.

This approach built trust, and employees experienced a strong sense of inclusion and support, even amid significant change.

When resistance arose, the company's dedication to customer-centricity provided a clear direction. They reminded themselves and their teams that every change was designed to improve customer service. This clarity kept the client and consultants aligned, particularly during critical moments when they needed to prioritize customer experience over short-term efficiency gains.

The outcome was a transformation process that, although challenging, resulted in greater employee engagement and minimal resistance compared to similar projects at other companies. The consultants, in turn, felt empowered to make honest recommendations without fearing negative consequences. Embodying its values throughout the project, the client accomplished its goals, reinforced its culture, strengthened employee loyalty, and improved customer satisfaction.

Weak Example: The Cost of Abandoning Values

Now, consider a different organization—a financial services firm that hired consultants to enhance operational efficiency. This company embraced values like integrity, employee well-being, and collaboration. However, when the consulting team suggested changes to streamline processes, the executive team focused on cost-cutting instead of these values, undermining employee morale.

One recommendation was to restructure the workflow to eliminate redundancy. This strategy involved shifting many responsibilities from experienced team members to junior staff. Although cost-effective, the consultants cautioned that this change could result in significant disengagement among the remaining senior staff. The organization's leadership dismissed these concerns, arguing that the financial savings outweighed potential morale issues. This decision directly contradicted the organization's stated values of employee well-being and integrity.

The fallout was swift. Senior employees began to disengage, feeling undervalued and unsupported, which reduced their performance and eventually led to turnover.

Employee morale declined as junior staff felt ill-prepared for their expanded roles, resulting in operational inefficiencies and client dissatisfaction. The consultants, whose recommendations were partially implemented but whose concerns were overlooked, struggled to salvage the situation. Eventually, the firm's leadership asked the consultancy to re-engage with a renewed focus on addressing employee disengagement—a problem that might have been avoided had the firm adhered to its core values from the start.

This failure to act on stated values compromised the project's outcomes, eroded trust in leadership, and left a lasting resentment beyond the consultancy period.

By ignoring its principles, the firm ultimately faced higher costs and enduring cultural damage that overshadowed any initial savings.

KEY VALUES ATTRIBUTES

1. Values Are the Foundation of Trust: An organization that exemplifies its values fosters trust, which is essential in consultative relationships. Trust empowers consultants to make innovative and candid recommendations, allowing the client to be open and receptive.

2. Values Guide Decision-Making Under Pressure: Values are compasses in challenging moments. When organizations depend on these values to direct their decisions, they help maintain alignment, prevent ethical compromises, and safeguard employee morale and stakeholder relationships.

3. Alignment Of Values Improves Outcomes: Aligning shared values benefits consultants and clients. It facilitates a smoother process, diminishes friction, and ensures all parties work toward a common goal.

4. Neglecting Values Has Real Consequences: Disregarding values, especially in challenging situations, can result in higher employee turnover, lower morale, strained relationships between consultants and clients, and subpar project outcomes. The costs usually outweigh any perceived benefits from short-term decisions that violate values.

5. Values Reinforce Organizational Culture: When organizations uphold their values, they strengthen their culture and positively impact employee engagement, customer loyalty, and brand reputation.

Values play a crucial role in shaping the success of consultative relationships. They serve as the threads that weave trust, integrity, and mutual respect between clients and consultants. Organizations that clearly define and consistently uphold their values foster a culture that promotes openness, ethical decision-making, and resilience under pressure. These qualities significantly impact the outcomes of consulting engagements, as values affect decisions and how they are executed and perceived by the broader organization.

Conversely, organizations that ignore or fail to act on their values risk undermining trust, eroding culture, and ultimately damaging their relationships with consultants. Such scenarios demonstrate that values are not optional niceties but essential to fostering productive, sustainable, and prosperous consulting outcomes.

Values guide the complex consulting world, where transformative change and tough decisions are often necessary. They align the organization with its consultants, ensure all stakeholders are respected, and provide a sense of continuity and purpose amid change.

Organizations that embody their values establish a foundation for long-term success, transforming consultative partnerships into powerful vehicles for growth and evolution.

EMPATHY

Empathy, the ability to understand and connect with the emotions, thoughts, and experiences of others, is a cornerstone of successful relationships in both personal and professional spheres. In organizations, empathy goes beyond individual relationships; it fosters collaboration, innovation, and loyalty. While many leaders acknowledge the importance of empathy, not all exemplify it effectively. This chapter examines empathy through real-world examples, highlighting strong and weak cases. Analyzing these contrasting examples uncovers the practices and principles that distinguish empathic organizations from those that do not meet the mark.

Let's discuss empathy from a consulting perspective. You're collaborating with someone who is your consultant; you are the client. Your consultant or team may need to convey something you might not want to hear. For example, your organization struggles to reach its desired future state, even when it seems attainable, could stem from actions you, as an organization or as a leader, are taking daily. These actions may feel right, but they can hinder the organization and block you from achieving your goals. You can't attain that desired future state because your actions undermine your chances of success.

Let's take a moment to reflect on this. It can be not easy to receive that message. It's tough to share such things with someone. Where does empathy fit in? If you want to be a good consulting client, consider the information the consultant or team provides and how challenging it might be for them to present it to you. Think about how hard it is for them to communicate things that may disrupt your self-image as a company leader. A good consulting client understands that while the news may be hard to hear, it can be just as hard to deliver. Take it a step further: when faced with unexpected news that contradicts your thoughts, being a good client means allowing empathy to take over and recognizing that this complex information is intended to benefit the organization. This is part of the consulting process, as you have hired or are collaborating with these consultants to receive candid, honest, and objective feedback or insights on what prevents you or your organization from progressing from the current state to your desired future state.

Empathy leads us to a familiar saying: don't shoot the messenger. Or receive the message without demonizing the person delivering it. That's a tough challenge.

If you've been working hard on your business to achieve results for your organization, and suddenly outsiders whom you barely know show up to tell you that the reason for your lack of success is that you aren't doing what you need to do or you're not doing it well, you can imagine that your ego and emotions would react strongly. It would not be easy to grapple with that, especially after years of dedication to your work.

Doing your best and working hard does not always mean working more intelligently; it often means putting in additional effort to achieve results that seem to elude you. The message you needed to hear might have arrived. While that message may not be easy to accept, approaching it with empathy— recognizing that complex messages can also be challenging to deliver—can position you as a great client for consulting. Being open and willing to listen to perspectives you may not have previously considered is crucial. As we've mentioned, if you aspire to be the organization you've never been, you're likely going to need to do things you've never done, think in ways you've never considered, and seek advice that you haven't received before or suggestions on how to move forward.

On the other hand, instead of being empathetic and understanding that this information, although possibly challenging to accept, is genuinely for your benefit and the benefit of the organization—which is essentially what you're investing in—the opposite reaction is succumbing to ego and emotion. This leads to a mindset that makes you a poor consulting client, where you begin to blame the messenger. You direct frustration toward the consultants, behaving as if they are there to insult or belittle you, making you feel small and inadequate in some way.

We've seen and worked with clients who lack the opportunity or need to develop empathy, which differs from the clients most consultants prefer to engage with.

This situation fosters a tense atmosphere where consultants might hesitate to share essential insights. They may hold back due to concerns about the client's reactions or lack of responsiveness.

This is not beneficial. Ultimately, you will miss out on the actual value of the consultative relationship if consultants refrain from communicating crucial information out of fear that you will react angrily, be harsh and dismissive, or attempt to undermine their expertise by implying they lack knowledge.

A good consultant considers these factors and shows empathy for what is being shared, even if it is unexpected.

The client who could benefit from better consulting often seeks to blame, deflect, defend, or discount the consultative advice, recommendations, or the reality of their current organizational state. This behavior contrasts with that of a good client.

Returning to our discussion, a good client understands that when they work with a consultant, they recognize that their current approach isn't practical.

They acknowledge that their past efforts could have been more successful. In other words, they realize that change is necessary.

We know only a few people who engage consultants who say, "No, we're just going to work with a consultant because we want to remain exactly as we are." Even if you're working with a consultant to seek validation, it is usually based on something you've accomplished. I rarely hear people asking consultants for validation before they have done anything.

Again, working with a consultant indicates that you're interested in making organizational changes, even if you still need to fully commit.

From that perspective, empathy is within reach when collaborating with a consultant because you focus on change and improvement.

Empathy shows that sometimes the best news can be the hardest to deliver, not just for the consultant conveying it but also for the business owner who has to accept or hear it.

EMPATHY: THE OVERLOOKED ELEMENT IN CLIENT RELATIONSHIPS

Empathy—the ability to understand and share the feelings or perspectives of others—can be just as elusive for consulting clients, particularly in high-stress, high-stakes projects. It is crucial for building trust, fostering a collaborative environment, and ensuring all stakeholders feel valued and understood. However, in consulting relationships, empathy is often overshadowed by a focus on results, metrics, and timelines.

Clients facing intense performance pressure may see consultants merely as tools for achieving targets rather than as partners in a shared journey of discovery and improvement. In some instances, clients need to fully appreciate the demands placed on consultants, including the need for adaptability and a genuine understanding of the client's cultural or operational context. A lack of empathy from clients can lead to friction, misunderstandings, and diminished motivation to bridge cultural gaps or adapt approaches to specific organizational dynamics.

Furthermore, clients who overlook empathy may fail to recognize the value consultants provide by understanding the human side of change. For instance, consultants frequently advise on sensitive issues like restructuring or cultural shifts, where empathy is crucial to secure employee buy-in and facilitate smooth transitions. Clients lacking empathy might prioritize efficiency over emotional intelligence, resulting in disengaged employees, resistance to change, and reduced project success.

In organizations where empathy is ingrained in the culture, leaders and teams are deeply committed to understanding and supporting each other's perspectives and challenges. Let's examine two examples of remarkable outcomes made possible by empathy.

A Global Tech Company's Approach to Restructuring

A major global tech company acknowledged the necessity of overhauling its business model and restructuring its workforce to remain competitive. This restructuring demanded significant alterations in job roles, redundancies, and relocations.

The company's leadership prioritized empathy, recognizing that such a transition could be emotionally challenging for employees.

Initially, leaders held empathy-focused workshops to better understand employees' anxieties, frustrations, and fears. They then met with team members at all levels to address concerns, clarify the reasons behind the changes, and encourage open feedback. Additionally, they provided personalized support, including career counseling, mental health resources, and flexible timelines for those needing extra time to transition.

Furthermore, the company established an internal task force to bridge empathy between employees and leadership. This group gathered ongoing feedback and modified transition plans based on employee needs.

For instance, the task force discovered that many employees were concerned about relocating to new offices, prompting the company to provide relocation stipends and flexible work arrangements.

As a result, employees felt heard, respected, and valued. Although restructuring was challenging, the company reduced resistance and fostered lasting loyalty.

Many employees, even those impacted by job cuts, expressed gratitude for the support they received and often departed with positive impressions, which enhanced the company's reputation.

A Retailer's Response to the COVID-19 Pandemic

When the COVID-19 pandemic disrupted daily life, a large retail chain showed empathy by prioritizing the well-being of both employees and customers. Acknowledging the heightened risk frontline workers face, the retailer quickly implemented new health protocols to create a safer work environment. They adjusted store hours for deep cleaning, reduced customer capacity limits, and installed plexiglass shields at cash registers.

But empathy extended beyond physical safety measures. The retailer provided employees with paid time off to address health concerns, mental health support services, and access to virtual healthcare. Additionally, the CEO and leadership team engaged with frontline workers through regular virtual meetings, listening to their experiences and adjusting policies as needed.

This strong display of empathy helped the retailer navigate the crisis while boosting employee morale and customer loyalty. Employees reported feeling supported and valued, which enhanced their commitment to the company during challenging times. Customers also recognized the company's caring approach, increasing sales and customer retention, even amid economic uncertainty.

Examples of Empathy Deficiency in Clients and Organizations

While some organizations recognize the value of empathy, others struggle to implement it effectively. A lack of empathy can result in disengagement, resistance to change, and a hostile corporate reputation. Here are two examples of situations where empathy was underutilized or completely absent.

A Manufacturing Company's Approach to Layoffs

A manufacturing company dealing with financial difficulties opted to lay off a significant part of its workforce.

While layoffs are sometimes unavoidable, how they are conducted can profoundly affect remaining employees, company culture, and public perception. Unfortunately, this company treated empathy as an afterthought.

The layoffs were announced abruptly in an impersonal email without prior consultation or explanation for the affected employees. Managers should have been permitted to discuss the layoffs with their teams beforehand, which has created a sense of betrayal among the staff. Furthermore, the company provided no support, counseling, or resources to assist the laid-off employees in transitioning to new roles.

Consequently, morale among the remaining employees sharply declined, productivity suffered, and distrust in leadership increased.

The company's lack of empathy in managing the layoffs harmed its internal culture and public image. Former employees expressed their frustration on social media, resulting in negative press coverage and impeding the company's ability to attract top talent in the future.

An Organization's Dismissive Response to Employee Feedback

In a large healthcare organization, frontline employees reported feeling overworked and unsupported due to increasing patient loads and limited resources.

However, when employees shared their concerns, leadership dismissed their feedback, attributing the complaints to a lack of resilience and adaptability. Rather than taking the time to understand employees' challenges, the leadership adopted a "tough love" approach, encouraging staff to "do more with less."

This dismissive attitude fostered resentment and resulted in high turnover rates, as employees felt undervalued and ignored. Patients also began to observe a decline in the quality of care due to staff shortages and heightened stress among the remaining workforce.

The organization's reputation suffered as word spread about the toxic environment, leading to a talent shortage. If the organization had shown empathy and responded to employees' feedback, it could have cultivated a more resilient and loyal workforce.

KEY EMPATHY ATTRIBUTES

1. Empathy in Practice: Empathetic organizations actively listen to the concerns of employees and customers, adjusting their actions to promote well-being and foster trust.

2. Employee and Customer Loyalty: Empathy builds positive relationships, enhancing loyalty and retention. Employees who feel valued and understood are likelier to stay engaged and committed.

3. Negative Consequences of Empathy Deficiency: Organizations that lack empathy experience lowered morale, high turnover rates, decreased productivity, and a damaged reputation.

4. Resilience Through Empathy: Companies prioritizing empathy are better positioned to navigate crises, as their employees and customers are more likely to support them during difficult times.

5. Leadership Responsibility: Effective leaders display empathy when recognizing others' perspectives and fostering safe environments where employees feel valued.

Empathy is an invaluable asset in today's organizations, fostering engagement, loyalty, and resilience. In this chapter, we examine how empathetic clients and organizations demonstrate the power of empathy by cultivating supportive and inclusive environments.

By examining real-world examples, we observed how empathy can lead to positive outcomes even in difficult situations, such as company restructuring and health crises. In contrast, a lack of empathy can cause decreased morale, lower productivity, and a weakened reputation.

The path forward is evident for organizations aiming to embed empathy in their culture. Leaders must actively listen, understand, and support the individuals they lead, recognizing that empathy is not a luxury but a fundamental pillar of organizational success.

In an increasingly complex and interdependent world, empathy is not just a value but a vital skill that allows organizations to thrive, adapt, and connect with the people they serve.

LISTENING

Listening is often underappreciated, yet it is pivotal in the consulting world. For clients, actively listening, thinking thoughtfully, and taking actionable steps based on what they have heard can transform consulting engagements and lead to impactful outcomes. This chapter explores how effective listening enhances client-consultant relationships and drives results. By contrasting examples of strong and weak listening, we can uncover the attributes of effective listening and understand why it remains a critical skill for all stakeholders in a consulting engagement.

Listening and hearing are similar yet distinct skills. Generally, hearing refers to the ability to perceive sound, while listening involves actively processing what you've heard, reflecting on it, and asking yourself, "Okay, now what?" We use a straightforward framework for listening that I share with clients. Whether they are consulting or executive coaching clients, it's this. Four key points should stand out when listening, particularly if you aim to be an effective consulting client.

As the consultant or consultants share information, you should first listen for "the what." What is it that they're trying to convey? What do they want us to understand or know? What is so important? What is the topic of conversation? We start with the "what." What is it?

The second thing to consider is the "so what?" Why is what they're telling us essential? What about their message makes me care? What indicates that we should care? Where's the importance? Where's the criticality? Where's the urgency? That's what I'm listening for. So what? We don't want to hear just anything; we don't want to listen to a story being told; we need to know what's significant about what we're hearing.

The third thing is, now what? What should we do with this information in the next 30 days? What should we do with this suggestion or recommendation now that we've taken it? Having listened for "the what" and "the so what," the next logical step in this model is, now what? What should we do with this? Are we supposed to take action? Or should we neatly fold this and put it on our mental bookshelf? Now, what is also time-sensitive? It is essential. You'd be surprised how often we attend meetings or have discussions with leaders, clients, or others, and they excel at telling us "the what" and "the so what." However, they leave it to us to determine what's happening now. As some say, without a call to action, it diminishes the significance of what we've just heard. Because if there's a strong "what" and a strong "so what," then the "now what" should also be equally compelling; tell me what we should do with this information right now.

Fourth and finally is then what. What are the action items and long-term goals? After initiating the current tasks, what are we supposed to do in the following weeks, months, or quarters? What will you have achieved following the actions today, this week, or this month? What follows next? What are the long-term efforts, the long-term considerations, and the long-term actions we need to take? Then what could happen anywhere from three to six months from now or even farther into the future? It addresses the question: if we do all of this, then what will occur? What are we expected to do? What defines the outcome? All of these elements are present. Again, to recap, you have "the what?" So what? Now what? And then what? If you're committed to being a good consulting client, you should listen for that.

When the consultant shares their findings with you—explaining why it's important, their recommendations for immediate actions, and, of course, their long-term suggestions—a good consulting relationship involves taking that information on board, perhaps writing it down, and then asking, how do we move forward with what we've been given? You don't just want to collect all this information; you need to absorb it and reflect on it. Absorbing the information is great. You can take in all this data, but then what? How often have you attended meetings where, in the end, you don't know what you're supposed to do with that? Or wonder if you even needed to be at this meeting. If you ever find yourself saying those things, it means someone didn't clarify the then what, so what, now what, and then what for you. They left that work for you to figure out. That's lazy behavior from whoever leads the meetings or acts as a consultant.

Yes, this book is about how to be a good consulting client. However, it also emphasizes that a good consultant should provide you with those four essential things so you don't have to search for them independently. What are we saying? If your consultant or consulting group isn't delivering those four things, ask for them. Demand those essentials because that's what a consulting engagement should achieve. You should address those four items so you can move forward independently, quickly, and in a manner that aligns with your organization's knowledge, skills, abilities, and bandwidth.

You can imagine the opposite: a complete refusal to listen to advice or suggestions. This often manifests in phrases like, "They need to know what they're talking about," or "This person needs to learn how to run my business; they struggle to understand what I do." It's easy to get on your high horse. Well, it's OK to be on your high horse, but ask yourself, is that horse moving? Is it galloping? Or is it just a statue going nowhere, waiting for you to propel it forward?

Ignoring advice undermines a good consultant-client relationship. Many consultants say, "Listen, we're here to offer our recommendations and suggestions, and that's our role."

If you come into this with the refusal to listen to whatever you hear, or if you've already decided that no one knows your business better, a consultant can't tell you what you should do, and you don't understand, what have you? That shut down, shut out mentality hinders reaching that desired future state. You may hear things when working with a consultant; you might listen to things you don't expect to hear about your organization. You may also hear things you're not prepared for regarding yourself as a leader in the organization, whether you're the owner, the founder, or otherwise. However, listening to someone who could be a better consulting client differs from the notion that they're not listening. In reality, a poor consulting client only listens to what they want to hear. In other words, they engage in selective listening. Those who are ineffective consulting clients pay attention only to what they want to hear, the things that make them happy, and the things that reassure them they have done everything correctly.

Suppose you've hired a consultant who shows keen interest and willingness to listen to you. Why not reciprocate by being open to the advice, suggestions, and recommendations of the consultants you're working with and incorporating them for your benefit? This idea of listening certainly goes both ways, but the best consultants are also the best listeners. Why do I say that? To wrap it up, it's a fact that if you're collaborating with consultants or a consulting group, and they've completed their preliminary analysis and due diligence, they go by various names. You'll notice that consultants ask more questions at the start of the engagement and make fewer statements during that time. Why? They want to understand you as a client, striving to grasp your business. That realization is genuinely compelling.

If you're working with a consultant who already knows the answer to your problem, they have a solution ready, and all they suggest is that you take what they've given you and plug it in, and away it'll go. You should be concerned. We would not hire that consultant; we'd run the other way. This suggests that the consultant or consulting group believes they understand your challenges well because they've encountered similar issues before. While they may have seen something comparable to your situation, this is their first time facing your specific problem. What do we mean? Through your listening, due diligence, and the consultant's listening and due diligence, you should arrive at a customized solution that connects specifically to your business, your leadership, and you as the owner, whoever may be reading this book. Whatever the solutions or the consultant's recommendations are, they should be grounded in this context and your business regarding its delivery stage.

How can you determine if you're working with a consulting group that genuinely listens? If the solutions they propose align with what you need and want from the consulting engagement, that's a good sign. If they don't, it indicates a lack of listening.

Similarly, a consultant who shares information but remains steadfast in your views suggests a fixed mindset. You might know precisely what you believe needs to be done and think your answer is the only one that counts. We encourage you to reflect on which behaviors indicate a good client. What behaviors would make you an effective consulting client? Is it your ability to listen and synthesize what you hear into solutions, recommendations, and pathways forward? Or is it preferable to be combative and reject any advice that doesn't resonate with you or doesn't come in the form you expect?

A consulting relationship can be thrilling. If you're dedicated to revisiting the book from a few years ago, you're also committed to the organization's values. If you're open-minded, you demonstrate that by listening.

LISTENING: A STRUGGLE TO HEAR BEYOND PRECONCEPTIONS

Listening is arguably one of the most crucial skills in any professional engagement, especially in consulting, where grasping the client's needs and context is essential. However, consulting clients often find it challenging to listen to insights and recommendations from external experts, particularly when these insights challenge their preconceived notions or established practices.

Clients frequently enter consulting engagements with inflexible expectations or a defined vision of their desired outcomes, which leaves little room for new ideas. This tendency is widespread when clients are committed to specific business practices or strategies they believe have been effective. As a result, even when consultants offer innovative perspectives, the client's unwillingness to listen can lead to lost opportunities and a hesitation to explore creative solutions.

Furthermore, ineffective listening can arise from the hierarchical structure within the client organization. Key decision-makers might inadvertently dismiss or filter feedback through an internal chain, leading to a lack of alignment among teams. This breakdown in communication across levels hinders collective understanding and strengthens the divide between consultants and client teams.

UNDERSTANDING THE IMPORTANCE OF LISTENING IN CONSULTING

At its core, listening in consulting is about understanding, aligning with, and responding to insights that may challenge preconceived notions, disrupt the status quo, or pave the way for growth. When clients listen effectively, they become more receptive to innovative approaches, better equipped to adapt to changing circumstances, and more likely to cultivate a culture of open-mindedness within their organizations.

Good listening fosters trust, enhances decision-making, and ensures that consultants' insights are acknowledged and transformed into meaningful action.

However, effective listening entails more than just hearing words; it requires analyzing the message, reflecting on it, and acting in accordance with it. In this section, we will examine two contrasting cases to illustrate how clients either excel in or struggle with these aspects of listening.

A Strong Example of Active Listening in a Client Relationship

Client Profile: A mid-sized manufacturing company undergoing a digital transformation, aiming to incorporate more advanced data analytics tools into its supply chain operations.

The Scenario: This company's leadership team recognized the need to modernize its supply chain. They partnered with a consulting firm to identify bottlenecks, enhance efficiency, and improve data flow to achieve this. While the leadership team had initial ideas for improvement, they intentionally engaged the consulting team to expand their perspective.

1. Attentive Engagement: During the initial discussions, the client listened actively to the consultant's perspectives, avoiding interruptions or premature assumptions. They encouraged the consultant to fully present their analysis before discussing initial ideas, showing an apparent openness to considering a new approach.

2. Thoughtful Reflection: The client should have responded more impulsively after the consultants presented their findings and recommended an advanced analytics platform for supply chain forecasting. Instead, they took time to discuss internally, posing critical questions that clarified potential outcomes, associated costs, and how the changes would align with broader strategic goals. This reflection period demonstrated that the client valued and took the consultants' input seriously.

3. Follow-Through on Recommendations: The client adopted the suggested analytics platform and invited the consultants to train their in-house team on how to use it. This follow-through ensured the initiative's sustainability and highlighted the client's commitment to implementing the advice they received.

4. Feedback Loop: The client communicated openly with the consultants throughout the implementation, offering feedback on successful elements and requesting adjustments as necessary. This feedback loop showcased a continuous commitment to listening and adapting to changing results.

The client's strong listening skills facilitated the successful integration of advanced analytics, reducing supply chain delays by 20% within the first six months. The client's attentiveness, thoughtful processing, and commitment to follow-through established a foundation of mutual respect, enabling the consultants to maximize their impact.

A Weak Example of Active Listening in a Client Relationship

Client Profile: A large retail chain experiencing declining sales in key product categories is seeking consulting support to revitalize its brand image and enhance customer engagement.

The Scenario: This client sought consulting expertise to revamp their branding strategy. The consultants identified several issues: an outdated digital presence, ineffective customer engagement practices, and a need for a refreshed product mix to attract younger consumers. However, the client had preconceived notions about the "real" problem— believing it was primarily an issue of an insufficient advertising budget—and wanted the consultants to concentrate on that aspect.

1. Interruption and Redirection: From the start, the client frequently interrupted the consultants' presentations, diverting the conversation to advertising expenses instead of letting the consultants tackle the core issues. This impatience prevented the client from fully

understanding the broader context of the recommendations.

2. Surface-Level Reflection: After the consultants proposed several comprehensive strategies, including rebranding, redesigning the website, and targeting a new demographic, the client initially seemed to listen but later resisted allocating resources to these areas. They briefly discussed the ideas internally but should have treated them more seriously.

3. Inconsistent Follow-Through: Despite initial assurances that they would implement several recommendations, the client only increased the advertising budget and made minor adjustments to their social media strategy. Still, they failed to follow through with more profound structural changes that would have produced sustainable results.

4. Lack of Feedback Loop: The client seldom provided updates or sought further input from the consultants, treating the engagement as a transactional exchange instead of a collaborative process. This absence of follow-up restricted the consultants' ability to adjust strategies or offer additional guidance.

The client's selective listening and failure to act on the consultants' key recommendations resulted in modest short-term sales improvements but no significant long-term change. Within a year, sales stagnated again, prompting the client to re-evaluate their approach and ultimately seek another consulting firm to tackle the same issues.

LISTENING KEY ATTRIBUTES

1. Attentive Engagement Is Foundational: Clients who listen without interrupting or redirecting allow consultants to share their insights fully. Attentive listening fosters a respectful environment that encourages open exchange and enables clients to understand the consultant's perspective thoroughly.

2. Thoughtful Reflection Enables Strategic Alignment: Clients who reflect on what they've heard appreciate the consultant's input. Reflection lets clients consider how proposed solutions align with their strategic objectives, resulting in more thoughtful and well-integrated decisions.

3. Consistent follow-through builds trust and drives results. Following through on recommendations or thoughtfully adapting them signals a client's commitment to change and

growth. Without action, listening becomes passive and unproductive, resulting in missed opportunities.

4. Feedback Loops Enhance Relationships and Promote Adaptability: By keeping open communication throughout the engagement, clients and consultants can refine strategies and react to real-time developments. Feedback loops prevent misunderstandings, foster alignment, and ensure both parties are involved.

In the consulting industry, listening is a cornerstone of success. Clients who actively listen, reflect carefully and follow through consistently are more likely to gain the full benefits of consulting engagements. They create a collaborative environment that allows consultants to leverage their expertise effectively and deliver lasting value.

Conversely, clients who struggle with listening— whether by clinging to preconceived notions, disregarding recommendations, or failing to implement suggestions—often miss out on transformative opportunities. Listening effectively is a soft skill and a strategic advantage that allows clients to engage with consultants fully, respond to industry changes, and unlock sustainable growth.

Ultimately, listening is an art that demands openness, patience, and commitment. Clients who excel in this skill will achieve their goals and establish more vital, resilient organizations ready to thrive in a dynamic business environment.

COMMUNICATION

Communication is the foundation for successful partnerships.

Effective communication aligns expectations, clarifies goals, and ensures transparency and focus on the relationship. This chapter explores the significance of active communication, highlighting both exemplary and challenging client cases to demonstrate its impact on consulting outcomes.

We will investigate how communication can accelerate or obstruct progress in consulting engagements by examining these contrasting examples. We will conclude with key takeaways for enhancing consulting interactions.

Consulting, change, and communication all start with the glorious letter C. A fourth C to consider is that they are all connected.

Hiring a consultant signals to others that you're willing to change how your organization operates and are open to changing how it implements its vision and mission. Working with a consultant suggests readiness for transformation. What ties all this together is the communication about the change, both to and through the consultant you are collaborating with.

Effective communication is essential in any business setting, business relationship, or personal relationship.

In this instance, to be an effective consulting client, you must be willing to communicate your needs and expectations to the consultant you work with. It is essential to ask for what you want and to express any tricky topics that may arise. You must also communicate your desires, voice your dislikes, and tell anyone you wish to exclude. Openness and timely communication are crucial.

It's not about saving everything for the best moment; that approach doesn't work. The essence of communication is real-time; some say it's simply time communication. To be an effective consultant-client, you should share with the consultants what is working and what is not. Be willing to discuss what you have done or what remains to be done to advance the consulting engagement. Eagerly share what you know or don't know about your organization so everyone can succeed. As noted, if you are genuinely interested in collaborating with a consultant, you will be open with them, sharing insights and understanding how improvements can be made.

A good client, on the other hand, needs to communicate. They must not withhold information, avoid sharing it in real-time, or completely disappear. Many consultants share stories about clients who suddenly become unresponsive. Sometimes, a client just ups and vanishes—not physically but from a communication standpoint. The client gives up. Perhaps it's because, until now, the client has heard things that don't make them happy.

We want to return to what we discussed earlier about listening and empathy. What the consultant has shared so far has led the client to say, "You know what? I'm not ready to listen to all of this right now. I feel wounded; it feels like days, weeks, months, and years of my time have been wasted. And I've just realized that I need some time to regroup—or even worse, I might not be interested in moving forward with this engagement anymore."

All of these decisions belong to the client. We're not saying the client can't or shouldn't take the time to say, "Listen, I need a timeout; I need to walk away for a bit."

All those things are the right thing to do. However, it doesn't benefit anyone when a client goes radio silent during a consulting engagement. Imagine a consultant working with a client who suddenly disappears. The consultant needs to know whether to continue, stop, or reassess. They wonder, "Did I say the wrong thing?" Those thoughts can creep in.

But what I find fascinating is that if you're working with a consultant, let's call them Consultant C, and you're committed to change, communication must be part of that process. If you are interested in the change you're seeking and hope to reach that desired future state away from your current situation, communication is the vehicle that will take you there.

A good consulting client understands that open lines of honest communication are essential to making things happen. Without that, only minimal change will occur during the consulting engagement without open, honest, and frequent communication.

THE COST OF MISALIGNED EXPECTATIONS AND AMBIGUITY

Clarity is vital for aligning expectations, setting goals, and ensuring a mutual understanding of project milestones and deliverables. However, poor communication is a common challenge faced when working with consulting clients.

Misaligned expectations, unclear requirements, and insufficient feedback can hinder even the most meticulously planned consulting projects.

Clients, for instance, may have ambitious goals but need to express them clearly, or they may expect consultants to interpret their implicit needs without explicit communication. This lack of clarity can create a disconnect between the consultant's approach and the client's expectations, leading to frustration. Miscommunication can also occur due to cultural or industry-specific jargon, where clients assume a level of expertise from consultants that might require additional context or clarification.

Some clients may withhold critical information due to confidentiality concerns, reluctance to reveal internal weaknesses, or a lack of communication infrastructure. With open lines of communication, consultants can often operate with complete information, making it easier to diagnose issues and develop tailored solutions accurately. The resulting frustration may breed resentment, as clients perceive the consultants as ineffective. In contrast, consultants believe they are set up to fail due to limited transparency.

THE ROLE OF COMMUNICATION IN CONSULTING

Communication extends beyond mere information exchange. Promoting mutual understanding requires active listening, thoughtful questioning, and proactive follow-through.

Communication connects vision and action for both consultants and clients. This dynamic is essential in consulting, where projects often feature complex, multi-layered objectives.

Clients who communicate effectively empower consultants to grasp their needs, anticipate potential challenges, and craft strategies that align with organizational realities. Effective communication in consulting encompasses:

1. Setting Clear Expectations: Both parties should fully understand the project goals, roles, and success metrics.

2. Ensuring Transparency: Being open about challenges and limitations allows for realistic planning.

3. Timely Feedback: Constructive criticism enables consultants to refine their recommendations and address changing client needs.

Although these components seem simple, they can often be challenging to implement.

To grasp the impact this can have, let's examine examples of clients who have demonstrated strong and weak communication practices.

A CLIENT WHO ACTIVELY COMMUNICATES AND FOLLOWS THROUGH

In this example, Alpha Finance, a major financial services firm, engaged a consulting team to help modernize its customer service operations.

From the outset, the leadership team demonstrated outstanding communication, offering a model of how client communication can improve consulting effectiveness.

Initial Engagement

During the onboarding phase, Alpha Finance's leadership proactively communicated its key objectives, detailing its short- and long-term goals for the project.

They offered detailed insights into current challenges, shared relevant documentation, and openly discussed earlier efforts to modernize that faced obstacles.

Alpha Finance's leadership ensured the consulting team understood the company's organizational structure and cultural nuances.

This context enabled the consultants to tailor their approach, making it practical and pertinent to Alpha Finance's specific needs.

Ongoing Communication

Throughout the project, Alpha Finance kept open lines of communication with the consultants. They held regular meetings and welcomed feedback and different perspectives. When consultants shared ideas or insights, the client team didn't merely listen—they asked clarifying questions, offered constructive criticism, and examined how each suggestion fit with their broader strategic goals.

Alpha Finance also demonstrated a strong commitment to follow-through. When the consulting team suggested workflow adjustments, Alpha Finance's leadership acted decisively by implementing pilot programs and collecting employee feedback. This iterative and responsive approach allowed them to avoid pitfalls and sustain momentum in their transformation efforts.

Outcome and Impact

By the end of the project, Alpha Finance had successfully integrated several new customer service technologies, restructured workflows, and achieved a measurable increase in customer satisfaction. Their proactive approach, thoughtful engagement, and prompt follow-through allowed the consulting team to work efficiently, saving time and resources.

The partnership reached its goals and surpassed expectations, establishing a benchmark for future consulting engagements.

A CLIENT WHO ACTIVELY COMMUNICATES BUT LACKS CONSISTENCY

Contrast Alpha Finance with a situation involving Beta Industries, a mid-sized manufacturing firm aiming to enhance its supply chain efficiency. Although Beta Industries was initially enthusiastic and communicative, challenges soon emerged that indicated a need for deeper engagement.

Initial Engagement

Beta Industries' leadership team enthusiastically launched the project, presenting an ambitious vision for supply chain transformation and organizing multiple meetings to discuss their goals.

However, these discussions often lacked specific details or thorough analysis of current operational issues. When consultants inquired about particular pain points or data to support the company's assertions, the responses were frequently vague or postponed to later phases, hindering the initial project momentum.

Communication Issues and Lack of Follow-Through

As the project progressed, communication issues became more apparent. Meetings with Beta Industries often devolved into discussions that revisited previous decisions or explored new, unrelated objectives.

This lack of focus made it difficult for the consulting team to maintain a steady course. They constantly adjusted priorities to align with the client's changing demands.

Additionally, Beta Industries struggled to follow up effectively. Although they acknowledged consultant recommendations during discussions, their actions frequently deviated from the agreed plan afterward.

For example, after a crucial decision to implement new supply chain software, the client did not allocate the necessary budget or resources, causing significant delays to the entire project.

Despite repeated reminders, the leadership at Beta Industries didn't fully commit to the changes, resulting in frustration and a lack of visible progress.

Outcome and Impact

Beta Industries' inconsistent communication and lack of follow-through hindered the consulting engagement's ability to deliver meaningful results.

Several recommendations were either poorly implemented or abandoned midway through the project.

Ultimately, the project fell short of its goals, and both sides recognized that the partnership had not fully realized its potential.

This experience underscored the importance of open communication, approaching it with clarity, commitment, and accountability.

COMMUNICATION KEY ATTRIBUTES

The contrasting cases of Alpha Finance and Beta Industries highlight essential principles of effective communication in consulting:

1. Clarity and Transparency: Clear and transparent communication enables accurate problem diagnosis and solution development.

2. Active Engagement: Clients who pose questions and challenge assumptions foster an insightful and collaborative process.

3. Consistent Follow-Through: Communication without follow-through leads to frustration and hinders progress. Successful clients act on insights and recommendations.

4. Focused, Goal-Oriented Dialogue: Regular meetings about project goals ensure effective time use and maintain momentum.

5. Adaptability and Responsiveness: Adapting and integrating new information while staying

aligned with the project vision ensures effective communication.

In consulting, communication goes beyond being merely a soft skill; it serves as a strategic asset that can dictate the success or failure of an engagement. Clients who communicate effectively cultivate a seamless and productive relationship, while those with clarity, consistency, or follow-through issues can diminish even the most effective consulting strategies.

Consultants should cultivate an environment that promotes transparency, establishes clear goals, and fosters mutual accountability.

Similarly, clients can enhance their investment by adopting a thoughtful and disciplined approach to communication from the initial engagement to project completion. By embracing these principles, both parties lay the groundwork for a successful

TRUST

Trust is fundamental to any successful consultative engagement. In consulting, trust encompasses more than simple confidence in the consultant's abilities; it requires a willingness to be vulnerable, a readiness to share sensitive information, and a commitment to a shared vision of success. Even the best strategies can falter without trust, as misunderstandings and misalignments can quickly derail a project. In this chapter, we will examine the role of trust in consulting relationships through examples of both strong and weak trust, outline the critical elements for establishing and maintaining trust, and conclude with actionable insights for building this essential foundation.

The interesting thing about trust, regarding hiring a consultant or being a good consulting client, is to abandon the preconceived notion some clients have that trust needs to be earned. Let go of the idea that trust must be earned. Instead, we'd like to propose a paradigm shift or a different way of thinking: Why not give trust until there's a reason to take it back?

For example, suppose you hire a consultant to help your organization transition from its current state to your desired outcome. To gain value from this relationship and be a good consulting client, you must trust that the consultants you've engaged have your best interests at heart. They are focused on the success of your business. This may not be easy to embrace and could require significant effort. You might think, "Before we hired this consultant, they knew nothing about us. They had to learn about our business; they didn't even know we existed. How can I trust someone meeting my business for the first time today? How can I trust someone who hasn't earned my confidence?"

The key differentiator between being a good consulting client and not lies in your ability to believe that the consultant is here to assess your organization objectively and help determine your next steps. Notice the word "could" ... what could be done to move you toward your goals?

What recommendations and suggestions will they provide? Can you trust that these recommendations are aimed at helping your business succeed and that they focus on your business's success? Exceptional consulting clients understand that they merge their expertise with the consultants. Didn't you mention earlier that you hire a consultant to bring in knowledge you lack? Yes, that's correct. When we refer to aligning your expertise with a consultant's, one crucial area of knowledge you possess, which your consultant does not, is your understanding of your business—specifically, your organization's origin story, culture, mission, and vision. These are aspects the consultant must learn from you before collaborating effectively.

That's why consulting often involves collaboration *with* the client, not just merely catering to the client's needs. It has to be collaborative. So, embracing that, if you can trust the consultant to learn from your expertise about your business and contribute their knowledge regarding the assistance you require, there's an opportunity for everyone to succeed in some way. Now, consider this: the consultant enters knowing they don't have all the answers about your business. They recognize that they need to learn what they can't see from you. Therefore, to help them grasp what they still need to know, you must be open to sharing information that, quite frankly, you haven't shared in the past. This information may feel uncomfortable for you to disclose, and it's something you'd prefer to keep private.

All of this is true, and we understand that some information may be hard to share. However, you are genuinely going to engage in the consulting process. If you are going to commit and invest in the success you desire, you need to combine your knowledge of your business with the expertise that the consultant brings from outside, which is why you are working with a consultant in the first place. A lot is happening here. To be a good consulting client, you must be willing to do that.

What does it look like when you're not a good consulting client? It involves being disrespectful, distrusting recommendations, and fighting the consultant tooth and nail against the advice, suggestions, and ideas they present. This behavior often stems from ego and emotion. If you sense a pattern here, you're on the right track. Ego and emotion obstruct the path to being a good consulting client. If you cannot release the preconceived notions about your past, present, or future success; if you struggle to let go of the emotions tied to hearing something you didn't want to hear; or if you're unable to accept that you haven't achieved the level of success you desired, it becomes challenging to be a good consulting client. This is because distrust can creep in. You may distrust the consultant because they do not say precisely what you want to hear; instead, they present a perspective that contrasts your expectations.

When we encounter clients who are, let's say, a nightmare for consultants... it's because every suggestion, recommendation, or idea presented in the conversation is met with distrust, skepticism, and the notion that you don't know what you're talking about. Therefore, the concept of trust is fundamental and transitions into the topic of honesty, which we'll discuss shortly in chapter seven.

THE ROLE OF TRUST IN CONSULTING

Consulting engagements often involve high-stakes situations, whether transforming organizational culture, addressing operational inefficiencies, or managing a central strategic pivot.

Since consultants are external agents who provide insights, strategies, and recommendations, clients must be willing to trust them deeply to achieve the best outcomes. Trust fosters openness, enabling consultants to access crucial information that might otherwise be withheld. It helps clients embrace recommendations—even those that challenge established practices. With trust, both parties can engage in honest discussions, take calculated risks, and support each other through the challenges of organizational change.

Strong Examples of Trust Between Consultants and Clients

1. Transformation Through Transparency

A leading retail company partnered with a consulting firm to revamp its customer experience and operations strategy after experiencing several years of declining sales.

To facilitate this transformation, the client provided standard financial reports and data on employee morale, customer complaints, and internal communications. This transparency demanded high trust, especially considering the sensitive nature of the issues discussed.

In turn, the consulting team reciprocated by giving candid feedback—even when it involved pointing out unflattering areas where the company had consistently underperformed.

The client demonstrated trust by accepting the consultants' recommendations and acting on them promptly. One of the recommendations involved significant restructuring in departments with a history of internal conflicts. The client's executive team feared this might lead to further disruption. Nevertheless, they proceeded, trusting the consultants' grasp of organizational dynamics.

This transparency and trust dramatically shifted the company's operations, enhancing morale and customer satisfaction scores.

The relationship, built on mutual respect and trust, allowed the consultants to facilitate a seamless and impactful transformation.

2. Trusting the Process with a Startup Client

A fast-growing tech startup enlisted consultants to refine its go-to-market strategy. Although the founders initially hesitated to share their financial projections and proprietary technology insights, they quickly understood the importance of transparency for the consultants to perform at their best. By building trust, they created a safe environment for open conversations about the company's strengths and weaknesses. This trust deepened as the consultants met expectations and showed adaptability, aligning with the company's unique culture and needs.

With trust established, the consultants introduced riskier yet potentially high-reward strategies. When the client expressed concerns, the consultants fostered open discussions. They addressed each point using data-backed insights and real-world examples. Ultimately, the startup embraced a bold new approach that propelled it into new markets. This example highlights how trust empowered both parties to pursue innovative solutions. The client's faith in the consultants' expertise enabled them to take calculated risks that would yield significant rewards.

Weak Examples of Trust Between Consultants and Clients

1. The Limits of Partial Disclosure

Consultants were hired to improve efficiencies, a government consulting project, and focus on streamlining public sector procurement. However, the government agency client was reluctant to share sensitive information about vendor relationships and existing contract structures, fearing disclosing information could expose unfavorable practices.

As a result, the consultants had to work with incomplete data, unaware of critical dependencies and potential risks in the procurement process.

With full disclosure, the consultants could formulate tailored recommendations, sometimes resulting in suggestions that were difficult to implement or missed the mark. This lack of trust led to subpar outcomes, and the project ultimately failed to achieve the expected efficiency gains. The client's reluctance to fully trust the consultants diminished the potential of the engagement, hindering the ability to create impactful change.

2. Trust Erosion Due to Unrealistic Expectations

A manufacturing company hired a consulting firm to reduce costs throughout its supply chain, as the CEO faced significant pressure to deliver results promptly.

However, instead of working collaboratively with the consultants, the executive team maintained strict oversight over every decision, consistently questioning the consultants' methods and recommendations. They hesitated to grant adequate access to key personnel and internal data, worried about leaks and disruptions.

The consultants' effectiveness could have been improved as they encountered these obstacles. The client's lack of trust resulted in micromanagement and strict control, hindering the consultants from exploring significant cost-cutting measures. Ultimately, the client prematurely abandoned the project, blaming the consulting team for "failing to deliver."

This fragile trust harmed the client-consultant relationship, resulting in wasted resources and an unresolved issue for the client.

KEY TRUST ATTRIBUTES

Through these examples, several crucial factors emerge as vital for building strong trust in consulting relationships:

1. Transparency / Openness: Sharing information openly allows consultants to offer the most tailored and practical recommendations. When clients completely disclose their challenges, consultants can develop strategies considering all variables.

2. Alignment on Goals and Expectations: Setting clear goals and realistic expectations allows both parties to pursue a shared vision, reducing misunderstandings and misaligned objectives.

3. Mutual Respect and Confidence: Acknowledging the expertise that both consultants and clients contribute fosters a respectful partnership. When clients believe that consultants prioritize their best interests, they are more likely to embrace and endorse recommendations.

4. Willingness to be Vulnerable: Trust necessitates that the client be vulnerable, share sensitive information, and must recognize their internal limitations. This openness enables consultants to address issues truthfully and precisely.

5. Commitment to the Process: Consulting engagements can bring uncertainty and change, which can be unsettling. Clients who trust the process, even amid initial discomfort or fear, are more likely to achieve transformational results.

Trust is a value and a cornerstone of effective consulting engagements. Strong trust between clients and consultants enables both parties to work openly, take calculated risks, and collaborate genuinely to solve problems.

Trust fosters the environment for innovation, honesty, and commitment, which are crucial for driving organizational change.

However, weak trust can limit the potential for meaningful outcomes, causing clients to withhold critical information, micromanage, or withdraw support too soon. When trust is compromised, both the consultant and the client struggle to achieve the full potential of the engagement, often resulting in unmet expectations, wasted resources, and strained relationships.

Investing in trust-building is crucial for both consultants and clients. This requires intentionally cultivating openness, transparency, and mutual respect. With trust as the cornerstone, consultants, and clients can collaboratively tackle even the most challenging projects, turning potential obstacles into shared successes.

Honesty

Honesty is the foundation of a productive and impactful consulting relationship. When clients and consultants are open and transparent with each other, they build a base of trust, mutual respect, and a shared commitment to the goals of the engagement. Without honesty, misunderstandings, missed opportunities, and frustration can lead to failed projects and damaged relationships.

This chapter will examine honesty in consulting engagements, providing examples that illustrate both the benefits of openness and the costs of dishonesty.

Honesty regarding what is communicated by the consultant and what is conveyed by the client to the consultant are the two essential bidirectional communication components. You must be honest about your starting point if you're committed to achieving a positive outcome as a good client.

In our research, we've observed that this is often the most challenging aspect for clients. We don't mean to suggest that clients are not paying attention or that they are disillusioned about their starting position as they strive to reach their goals; rather, we believe that too often, they are so focused on their own business that they fail to take the time to assess their standing relative to competitors, the industry, and their objectives. There's nothing inherently wrong with concentrating on your own business.

For instance, you're an organization that has hired a consultant for several years. You've been working to build that business and organization, and now you've reached a point where, despite your best efforts, you can't move forward any longer. You're not making progress anymore. The idea of being a good client is to be honest about what you've tried, what has worked, what hasn't worked, what you have done and not done, and where your points of failure are—both anticipated and realized—whether you've received feedback in some way. Being honest with yourself as a good client about your current situation is essential to getting started. As you've heard me say, it's all about reaching the desired future state. Well, transitioning from your current state is how that happens.

If a client is not honest with the consultant about their starting point, it could set the consultant up to repeat past mistakes or potentially revisit unsuccessful strategies. This might lead to the consultant wasting time trying to reach an unreachable destination because the starting point has not been established properly. For example, one could use the analogy: "As our desired future state, we aim to be in Las Vegas on the Las Vegas Strip at the Cosmopolitan Hotel, but specifically at roulette table number five in the casino by 6 p.m. Eastern tonight."

If that's where we want to go, don't we have to figure out where we are? That will dictate our path, method of transportation, and everything else. If you are already in Las Vegas and starting on the other side of town, closing the gap between where you want to be and where you could be is relatively simple. You need to know the local traffic patterns. You have to think about when you want to leave, how much time you need to give yourself, etc. But what if your starting point is in Amsterdam? Suppose that's where you are, and you want to be at the Cosmopolitan Hotel's roulette table number 5 on the Strip in Las Vegas by 6 p.m. Eastern tonight. In that case, you have many other factors to consider, like time zones, transportation, and money.

All these different factors come into play. From an honest standpoint, to illustrate a point, if a consultant needs to understand where the organization is genuinely starting from, how can they propose solutions to help the organization reach its goals? What if the consultant creates a plan to get the client from Amsterdam to Las Vegas when, in reality, the client is already in Nevada? This situation is challenging because the client hasn't been truthful about their starting point.

And let's face it, the client must know where they're beginning. I've experienced this firsthand, where a client has raised their hands and said, "Listen, I don't know what's going on. I don't know what's not working. I don't know why it's not working, but I need help."

If the client needs to know where they're starting or hasn't been honest with the consultant about their position, the consultant could waste time and create something unnecessary and unimpactful that won't deliver the expected results. Therefore, the concept of honesty in the consultant-client relationship is essential.

It is being willing to share information about trust, as we mentioned in Chapter 6. You must ignore the "You only get my trust if you earn it." Instead, move toward, "I give you my trust until you give me a reason not to trust you, and be open and honest with where we're getting started in this consulting engagement."

Yes. It could be embarrassing, or we could have an uncomfortable conversation about where we are starting from and, more importantly, how we got here. But that's what we need to have in an actual consulting engagement.

The most outstanding consulting clients are willing to be open and honest about what has been done, what has been thought, what has been said, what has been tried, and what has failed. If that openness is lacking, it indicates that the client may not be a good fit for consulting, as dishonesty deprives us of the opportunity for success.

We honestly don't mean to imply that lying is involved when we say this. We're not referring to mere embellishments or outright falsehoods. Sometimes, dishonesty occurs through omission. The client might need to inform the consultant about our starting point. They feel like we're playing a strange game. Let's see how skilled this consultant really is. Let's see if they can uncover where we've been and what we've accomplished. That's similar to mind reading. Unfortunately, no one we know is a certified mind reader. Consultants aren't mind readers; we ask questions.

We are the folks who can help you determine where you're going based on where you've been. But if we need to know where you've been, how can a consultant help you figure out where you are going? The short answer is that they can't. You might come up with some presuppositions, but they could be completely wrong, which helps no one. So, honesty is key. A good client is honest about what has happened and what has gone right. If there's any sense that you can't be open, that you can't be truthful, or that you can't be transparent—there's the word—if you can't be transparent with the consultant you're working with, you're already on the path to not necessarily being a good client. This means you're on the road to not getting the desired results from your efforts.

Consultants are often blamed for failing to deliver what clients want. The shame is that if the client had been more honest about their background and what brought them to their current position, the consultant could have provided a better analysis and a clearer picture of the path from here to there. Again, as we mentioned, the best client understands that they are working with their consultant, not that the consultant works for them.

It's an exciting paradigm based on the idea that as a good consulting client, you're there to collaborate with the consultant. It needs to be a partnership. There must be a connection and a willingness to fully commit to achieving the desired results. Without that commitment, you're likely to face disappointment.

Strong Example of Honesty: Navigating Change with Transparency

One of the most compelling examples of honesty in consulting occurs when clients candidly share their challenges, even if they are sensitive. For instance, a large healthcare organization hired a consulting firm to help improve patient satisfaction and streamline operations. Initially, the client's executive team was reluctant to discuss specific issues, fearing judgment or potential repercussions. However, recognizing that a lack of transparency would hinder the consulting team from fully grasping the problems, the CEO deliberately chose to be completely honest.

The client disclosed several significant, previously hidden issues: a high employee turnover rate, widespread dissatisfaction among nursing staff, and conflicts between administrators and medical professionals. Although the organization's leaders felt uncomfortable sharing these details, they acknowledged that complete transparency was the only way for the consultants to truly assist them. This openness enabled the consultants to customize their approach, creating targeted solutions that tackled the underlying causes of low patient satisfaction.

The consulting team introduced programs to improve employee engagement, provided leadership training to managers, and established forums for medical staff to express their concerns. This customized approach improved patient satisfaction and created a healthier workplace culture. The CEO later acknowledged that, had the leadership team not been genuine, the consultants would likely have suggested more generic solutions that would have fallen short. This example demonstrates how honesty enables consultants to dig deeper and create lasting change.

<u>Weak Example of Honesty: Concealing Financial Challenges</u>

In contrast, dishonesty or a lack of transparency in consulting engagements can lead to serious consequences. A manufacturing company hired a consulting firm to streamline operations and reduce costs. Initially, the client insisted that their financial situation was stable despite internal concerns about the company's imminent cash-flow crisis. The client worried that revealing their financial instability might prompt the consulting team to suggest drastic measures that could upset employees and investors.

Assuming the company's finances were solid, the consultants focused on operational efficiencies and productivity improvements, suggesting changes that needed extra investments in new technology. However, as the project progressed, the truth about the company's financial struggles emerged. Given the company's limited resources, the consultants quickly realized their recommendations were impractical.

It was too late when the consultants changed their approach to recommending emergency cost-cutting measures and cash-flow management strategies. The client's financial position had already worsened, and the company ultimately had to file for bankruptcy within months of the project's conclusion. This situation might have been avoided if the client had been truthful about their financial circumstances. The consultants could have prioritized immediate actions to stabilize cash flow rather than suggesting long-term investments the company couldn't afford.

Mixed Example of Honesty in Culture Change Efforts

In some cases, clients provide partial truths that, while not outright lies, still lead to suboptimal results. For example, a technology firm hired a consulting team to enhance its workplace culture, citing a need for improved collaboration and innovation. The client shared many of the challenges they encountered, such as siloed departments and a high rate of employee burnout. However, they should have included a key detail: several senior leaders resisted change and actively discouraged new ideas from junior staff, fearing that these changes could undermine their authority.

Even though the consultants devised a comprehensive culture change strategy emphasizing cross-departmental projects and innovation workshops, the initiative encountered significant roadblocks. The consultants lacked clarity regarding senior leaders' need for greater buy-in, which stalled progress.

When the reality of the leadership resistance finally emerged, the consultants had to adjust their approach. They spent more time coaching senior leaders and securing their commitment to the change. If the client had been sincere, the consultants could have addressed leadership issues, making the cultural transformation smoother and more effective.

Key Honesty Attributes

1. Honesty as a Foundation for Tailored Solutions: Full transparency enables consultants to grasp the entire context, resulting in customized solutions that tackle root issues instead of just symptoms.

2. Consequences of Concealment: When clients hide essential information, consultants may provide recommendations that do not align with organizational needs or constraints. This frequently leads to ineffective results and wasted resources.

3. Limitations of Partial Honesty: Even slight omissions can impede the success of a consulting engagement. Addressing all challenges openly, even when uncomfortable, is crucial for a realistic and sustainable strategy.

Honesty is crucial for a thriving client-consultant relationship. The examples presented here illustrate that honesty may sometimes feel uncomfortable, but it is ultimately in the client's best interest. When clients are transparent, consultants can deliver targeted, impactful solutions. Conversely, when clients withhold or distort information, they jeopardize the project's success and risk undermining the trust and goodwill between both parties.

By embracing honesty, clients empower consultants to become genuine partners in addressing their most pressing challenges. Consultants can provide deeper insights, recommend more effective strategies, and facilitate meaningful, sustainable change in a relationship founded on honesty and transparency.

ENTHUSIASM

Enthusiasm is a powerful catalyst for success in any professional relationship, but it is particularly influential in consulting.

When clients and consultants share a genuine passion for the work, the project is more likely to thrive, overcoming challenges and delivering innovative solutions. Enthusiasm fuels engagement, drives collaboration, and fosters a positive, forward-thinking, forward-looking atmosphere. Conversely, lacking enthusiasm can lead to disengagement, misalignment, and missed opportunities.

In this chapter, we examine the role of enthusiasm in the consulting relationship, illustrating both strong and weak examples while offering strategies for cultivating enthusiasm.

Enthusiasm is a vital element of being a good consulting client. Most clients reported that they are good clients who express enthusiasm and gratitude for the chance to work with a consultant—not from a perspective of gaslighting or attempting to overly inflate the consultant's confidence, but not necessarily based on what was explicitly said.

There are many ways to express enthusiasm, such as being available to the consultant when the client says they will be. This can be reflected in their correspondence, whether through email or back-and-forth communication, in discussions during meetings when they occur, and in demonstrating gratitude as a person who shows excitement for moving toward their desired future state.

The idea of enthusiasm is powerful. It is widespread to see a consultant who seems genuinely excited about their work with the client, enthusiastic about the job's outcome, and excited about the direction they're taking. They are just happy that they're no longer in this place they were in. They have this desired future state and might have felt stuck in their current situation for a considerable time. However, the arrival of a consultant signals that we will be transitioning from the current state to or toward that desired future state.

Sometimes, a consultant's advice, counsel, or recommendations may be far-reaching or, in some cases, off-putting to the client—not due to what was said, but because the client is coming to realize that their previous actions may not have been practical. This realization can begin to diminish a client's enthusiasm.

For example, a client has spent several months or even years working in a certain way, wondering why they have been unable to move forward and achieve the desired success or results. They decide to work with a consultant, embarking on that path enthusiastically, excited about the opportunities ahead. Yet, somewhere along the way, they realize that their lack of success stems from the very actions they have been taking.

Enthusiasm may start to wane, and destructive behaviors could emerge. Another factor to consider carefully is that as we progress toward that desired future state, the client sometimes realizes that significantly more work is required than they anticipated or are prepared to undertake. Because of this, the level of enthusiasm can fluctuate. It makes sense that someone may have an idealized vision of what needs to happen, when, and how. A consultant arrives and, through their due diligence, preliminary analysis, and all the typical tasks a consultant would perform, reveals to the client that the path they believed they would follow is steeper than they had imagined.

One of the factors that can dampen enthusiasm is the initial stage of the journey. We have witnessed enthusiasm flourish in clients as they dive deeper into their work and realize how to get closer to their goals and tackle some of their challenges. We've also noticed that clients who start with less enthusiasm often become more passionate when they see the proverbial light at the end of the tunnel. Thanks to this consultative support, they engage more and show greater involvement in the process because they start to believe that what initially seemed complicated and impossible may not be so difficult. Therefore, many aspects contribute to fostering enthusiasm.

However, many consultants believe that the most critical element is when a consultant can collaborate with a client who is engaged, present, eager to learn, and willing to partner with the consultant rather than making the consultant work solely for them. This mutual enthusiasm enhances the experience. An enthusiastic consultant is often paired with a passionate client, which significantly improves engagement.

This alignment increases the likelihood that outcomes will closely meet the client's expectations, making what could be a daunting challenge feel much more manageable.

Strong Example of Enthusiasm in a Consulting Relationship

Consider the situation of a major retail company that engaged a consulting firm to revamp its digital marketing strategy. The client had been experiencing stagnation in online sales and was keen to refresh its approach in a competitive marketplace. From the beginning, the client's leadership team displayed notable enthusiasm for the project, seeing the consultant as a valuable ally in realizing their vision. This enthusiasm manifested in several ways:

1. Active Engagement: The client team actively brainstormed sessions, offering feedback and sharing insights about the company's unique challenges. Rather than merely receiving solutions, they contributed ideas and openly discussed potential roadblocks with the consultants, eager to co-create the best strategy.

2. Commitment to Innovation: The consultant's suggestions thrilled the client, especially incorporating advanced data analytics to tailor marketing strategies. While this approach was novel, leadership was eager to experiment with cutting-edge technologies to maintain a competitive edge.

3. Celebrating Success: As the project advanced, the client and consultants acknowledged small victories, such as improved engagement metrics from initial test campaigns. This joint celebration strengthened their enthusiasm and energized the project's momentum.

The consultants were motivated by the client's enthusiasm, prompting them to delve deeper into their business and apply their expertise to create customized, innovative solutions. Consequently, the project not only met but surpassed expectations, resulting in the client seeing a substantial rise in online sales and market share.

This example illustrates the impact of a positive and enthusiastic atmosphere. The client's excitement was infectious, inspiring the consultants to put more energy, time, and creativity into the project, leading to a highly successful outcome.

Weak Example of Enthusiasm in a Consulting Relationship

Contrast this with the experience of a consulting firm hired by a manufacturing company to enhance its production processes. The client had a clear goal: boost efficiency and lower operational costs. However, the client's enthusiasm was tepid, bordering on indifference.

1. Lack of Engagement: Although the client sought to enhance performance, they needed to be fully committed. They assigned the project to mid-level managers, who had to grasp the strategic significance of the transformation. This required greater involvement from senior leadership, and the client needed to allocate time for in-depth discussions with the consultants.

2. Resistance to Change: The consultants suggested implementing lean manufacturing techniques that could transform the client's operations. However, the client's excitement was dampened by their hesitance to change. They were used to their current processes and were concerned about the disruption to their daily operations. The leadership team's lack of enthusiasm fostered an atmosphere of skepticism, which impeded the consultants' ability to advocate for the changes.

3. Unclear Communication: The infrequent, often vague communication complicated the issues. The client's feedback lacked specificity and consistency. Although there was excitement about potential improvements, the absence of shared information slowed progress; the client's sense of urgency and enthusiasm dwindled, affecting the consultants' approach. They began to doubt whether their ideas would be embraced. They found it difficult to maintain the same level of commitment. Consequently, there were only marginal improvements in efficiency, and the client could not fully capitalize on the potential of the consultants' recommendations.

ENTHUSIASM KEY ATTRIBUTES

1. Enthusiasm, or its absence, plays a crucial role in determining the success of client engagements. When clients show enthusiasm, it can result in:

2. Enhanced collaboration: Clients are more inclined to engage actively in the consulting process, providing valuable insights and feedback that result in more customized solutions.

3. Motivation and activity: Enthusiasm inspires client consultants to think creatively, take risks, and explore innovative approaches.

4. Positive momentum: Shared enthusiasm generates energy and momentum, aiding the project's advancement despite challenges.

On the other hand, weak enthusiasm leads to:

Disengagement: When clients lack enthusiasm, consultants may need help to gain buy and not fully embrace their shift in excitement, which can create resistance, as clients might hesitate to implement new ideas or challenge existing processes.

Missed Opportunities: A lack of enthusiasm often results in missed chances for deeper collaboration, more effective problem-solving, and higher-impact outcomes.

Enthusiasm is not just a positive trait; it's a critical factor influencing the trajectory of a consulting engagement.

For a project to succeed, the client and the consultant must be energized, aligned, and excited about the potential for change. Enthusiastic clients create a collaborative and innovative environment, motivating consultants and encouraging deeper involvement and creative problem-solving.

On the other hand, weak enthusiasm can lead to disengagement, resistance to change, and less-than-optimal outcomes. By recognizing the confidence level in a client relationship, consultants can adapt their strategies to promote greater involvement and excitement, ultimately ensuring the success of the engagement.

Fostering enthusiasm should be a priority for consultants and clients from the initial meeting to the project's final stages. When both parties are fully engaged and passionate about the work, the potential for transformational success is limitless.

PRESENCE

"Presence" encompasses emotional and physical engagement in conversations or meetings.

A consultant's presence can significantly influence relationship dynamics with the client, shaping the trajectory of a project and the effectiveness of proposed solutions. Being present involves actively listening, demonstrating empathy, and staying attuned to the client's intellectual and emotional needs.

This chapter explores the importance of presence in consulting engagements, providing examples of how it can elevate or hinder the outcomes of consultative interactions.

If the client is willing and ready to objectively examine their organization and allow what some might refer to as a stranger to observe the internal dynamics, they can begin to receive thoughts, insights, and recommendations. This requires presence. It takes a certain openness from the client to engage with these aspects. The client's willingness to perceive the business and its realities as they are in the moment is essential, along with a healthy mindset to facilitate this Process.

So, what does a healthy mindset entail? It means being able to view a situation through different perspectives. Can you see the business, the problems, and the challenges through someone else's lens? That mental presence is critical, as is physical presence. There have been many cases where a client has hired a consultant and asked for assistance, but then the consultant finds themselves following a path mapped out for and with the client, only to realize the client is unavailable, disinterested, or missing in action. They may struggle to find time for meetings, conversations, or even returning emails and phone calls. It becomes difficult for a consultant to partner with a client who expects to dictate the initial order for what they want and then disappear, waiting for the consultant to deliver on their requests. It doesn't function that way.

In many instances, the reality is that a consultant collaborates with and for the client, not just for them. To successfully work together, the client must be engaged. Many consultants have noted that projects can drag on or become overly complicated due to the client's absence or unavailability.

If a client who doesn't attend meetings sends a message to the consultant stating that even though I'm paying for the consultant's time, that time could be more valuable. We know that no one likes to have their time wasted. Why? Time is one of the most expensive resources known to humankind, and none of us are getting any more of it. We don't know how much we have; we must recognize when our time is up. So, even though a consultant may be working with a client on what we commonly call billable hours, the concept of presence is critical when considering that the client aims to achieve a specific result, outcome, or deliverable. If the client is not willing to be present and collaborate with the consultant to reach that goal, and if they are not ready to invest the time to be available, then it indicates to the consultant that while the client may desire an outcome or a set of deliverables, they may unfortunately not be willing to take the necessary steps to achieve that.

Another aspect of presence that relates back to enthusiasm is that during a consulting engagement, a good client will understand that there will be work required from them after the engagement. Clients lacking a healthy sense of presence may be surprised that the work begins after the engagement concludes and the contracted months are up.

After the consultant has completed their role with the organization, the client typically implements the outcomes. We've often discussed the various components of a consulting engagement.

A consultant aims to comprehend the client's needs during any consulting engagement. In other words, what is the significance?

What is the urgency? What motivates clients to pursue this for their business, themselves, or industry? What have you accomplished? What are the key components of the consulting engagement?

The consulting engagement begins to close when the consultant and the client arrive at the 'now what' stage. In other words, what will occur immediately after this consulting engagement once we've explored the "what" and the "so what?"

So, what happens next unless the client has paid for or engaged the consultant to execute what's outlined in the consulting engagement? Typically, the results belong to the client, and now that we've accomplished all of this, it means, okay, client, we've developed an action plan and next steps. The next steps belong to the client, which outlines what they will do in the next 30, 60, and 90 days to move toward their desired future state. What will the client do after the first 30, 60, or 90 days? How will they maintain the momentum? How will they ensure their success continues? Many have noted that it takes at least 30 days or longer for new habits or practices to become standard for an organization or individual, similar to going to the gym or starting an exercise regimen.

It takes two to three weeks, maybe even four weeks, of repetition to get into the mindset and flow of incorporating this new approach into one's schedule, agenda, etc. So, what is the client ready to tackle in this presence aspect? Typically, when the consulting engagement ends, there's a transition period known as the transference of ownership, where the client takes ownership of the consulting engagement and shifts from a consulting project to a consulting program that requires execution by the client.

In many cases, the client may contact the consultant for help or guidance: What did you do while executing the action plan? However, the focus is now very deliberately on the client's presence, their willingness to move forward, and hopefully, drawing from the previous chapter, the enthusiasm needed to persevere. As the client executes the action plan developed collaboratively with the consultant, there will inevitably be times when they face significant challenges to progress.

There may be some unexpected inclines. Businesses are dynamic. Various factors can distract the client from their work or extend the timeline for deliverables. Many different elements are in play, with numerous other components to consider. Therefore, the concept of presence is: Can the client be engaged at the beginning, during, and after the consulting engagement?

The Dual Aspects of Presence: Emotional and Physical

Presence, in the context of consulting, can be broken down into two primary dimensions:

1. Emotional Presence: This involves being attuned to the client's emotional state and understanding their concerns, motivations, and challenges. It requires empathy and the ability to engage on a human level. Emotional presence enables consultants to connect deeply with clients, fostering trust and rapport.

2. Physical presence refers to the physical aspect of engagement. It includes maintaining eye contact, being fully present in the moment, and minimizing distractions. It also encompasses nonverbal cues that convey attentiveness and respect, such as body language, posture, and facial expressions. Physical presence signals to the client that the consultant values their time and input.

A consultant must combine emotional and physical presence to be effective in a consultative setting.

Let's examine what this looks like in practice through examples.

Strong Example of Presence: A Consultant Fully Engaged

Imagine a consultant named Alyssa meeting with the CEO of a tech company to discuss implementing a new software system. As the CEO shares concerns about the system's potential impact on employee morale, Alyssa listens intently, leaning slightly forward. Her eyes are focused on the CEO, and she nods occasionally to indicate that she is absorbing the information. She refrains from interrupting, allowing the CEO to express her thoughts fully.

Emotionally, Alyssa is fully engaged. She senses the underlying anxiety in the CEO's voice and the tension in their body language. Once the CEO finishes speaking, Alyssa acknowledges the emotional weight of the concerns, saying, "It sounds like you're worried not just about the technical implementation but about how this will impact your team's culture. That's a valid concern, and we should address it upfront." Her empathetic response validates the CEO's feelings, establishing trust and rapport.

Alyssa's physical presence is also evident. She avoids distractions, her phone is off, her body language is open and welcoming, her posture attentive, and she maintains steady eye contact, signaling to the CEO that she values their perspective and is fully engaged in the conversation. This emotional and physical presence mix helps Alyssa better grasp the CEO's concerns and establishes a strong basis for a collaborative solution.

Weak Example of Presence: A Consultant Disengaged

In contrast, consider the example of another consultant, John, who is meeting with a senior manager at a manufacturing company. As the manager starts outlining operational challenges, John listens but appears distracted. He periodically glances at his watch and checks his phone under the table; his responses are brief. While the manager discusses issues related to employee turnover, John seems more focused on his notes than on emotionally engaging with the speaker.

John's physical presence appears weak. His posture is closed, his arms crossed, and he avoids eye contact with the manager. He remains reclined rather than leaning in or nodding to show engagement, which signals a lack of interest or attentiveness. This creates a disconnect between the consultant and the client.

On the emotional front, John fails to notice the frustration and stress in the manager's voice. He doesn't acknowledge the emotional aspects of the conversation, leaving the manager feeling unheard and unsupported. John's responses are pragmatic, focusing on the technicalities of the situation but overlooking the human element. For instance, he might say, "Well, we can reduce turnover by implementing more rigorous hiring practices," without ever addressing the emotional toll turnover takes on the team's morale.

PRESENCE KEY ATTRIBUTES

The contrast between Alyssa's and John's approaches highlights several key points about presence in consultative interactions:

1. Emotional Engagement is Key to Trust: Clients must feel emotionally understood. Recognizing their fears, challenges, and frustrations builds trust. It shows the consultant cares about their success, not just closing deals.

2. Physical Presence Enhances Connection: Consultants who make eye contact, minimize distractions, and use open body language fosters a positive environment where clients feel respected and heard. These physical cues indicate that the consultant is fully present and focused on the conversation.

3. Active listening is essential: True listening goes beyond merely hearing words; it involves actively processing shared information, asking clarifying questions, and engaging in reflective responses that show understanding.

4. Balancing Both Aspects is Critical: A consultant who is physically present but emotionally distant (like John) or emotionally involved but physically distracted falls short. Both emotional and physical presence must function together to establish a successful consultative relationship.

The importance of presence in consulting cannot be overstated. It directly affects the quality of client relationships and the success of projects.

Consultants who are emotionally and physically present establish stronger rapport, build trust, and create a collaborative environment that promotes problem-solving. Conversely, when consultants do not engage fully—whether due to emotional detachment or physical distraction—they risk alienating clients, overlooking critical insights, and ultimately failing to achieve meaningful results. To be genuinely effective in consulting, professionals must develop emotional and physical presence.

This necessitates self-awareness, attentiveness, and a sincere interest in the client's concerns. When consultants are fully present, clients feel heard, respected, and supported, leading to more productive engagements and improved outcomes.

WILLINGNESS

In any consulting engagement, willingness is crucial in determining the potential for success.

Whether in leadership development, organizational transformation, or process optimization, the client's readiness to collaborate with the consultant can shape the direction and outcomes of the entire project. Genuine, holistic willingness is not just about agreeing to hire a consultant; it involves a mindset of openness, trust, and a commitment to working together to

This chapter will examine the concept of willingness in consulting engagements, offering strong and weak examples to illustrate the contrasting outcomes. We will also analyze the components of authentic, holistic willingness. We'll conclude with the key takeaways that can steer consultants and clients toward more productive and rewarding partnerships.

The critical question is whether the client will be willing to adapt their expectations if a different solution is proposed than they initially anticipated. So, what does that entail? If the client enters the consulting engagement expecting mere validation, they should expect the consultant to align with the client's preconceived notions or hidden (or not-so-hidden) agendas. Is the client prepared to take a different direction if that is the consultant's recommendation? Again, we assume the consultant is there to help the client achieve their desired outcome. This means it will require considerable effort. It doesn't imply that the client will readily accept the consultant's proposal. The client may need to swallow their pride, revisit their schedule, and question, "Do I want to follow this consultant's advice?" In other words, "What I expected to happen is now not happening, and I need to recalibrate. I need to pause and reflect on this for a moment. I need to recommit if it may differ significantly from the consultant's suggestion."

Willingness often means a willingness to adapt; now, the back of the coin for this one is that, in certain instances, the client may look at what must be done and lose all desire to move forward. And that turns into stalled projects and a lack of progress. Some might refer to it as a failure to launch. One might wonder why a client would engage a consultant and invest the time, energy, and money required only to reach the end and think, "I'm not willing to do this." It certainly seems like a waste of resources. Yet, the reality is that working with a consultant can be challenging, even intimidating, for some. It's scary because it involves undoing previous work. It may also involve a shift in someone's identity. This concept ties back to the idea of willingness. Am you prepared to be the organization leader or the business owner you want to be? Need to be? You may have to learn to become the business owner you've never been before, necessitating the willingness or desire to undertake tasks that haven't been done before. This is an exciting dynamic that many consulting clients must reflect upon. How can I cultivate a mindset willing to pursue what I've never done?

What must you do as a client to create an environment where the consultant can recommend all the components for success and where you are willing to engage with those suggestions because you believe the necessary work is appropriate? After all, it's in service of a desired outcome. So, what does it mean to be a good consulting client? Does it mean entering a consulting engagement with eyes wide open?

No.

Collaborating with an engaged client is the key to achieving the results and outcomes they desire. Why? Consultants don't work for the client; they work alongside the client. The most successful clients understand this and keep it in mind.

The best consulting clients embody everything we've discussed. They take the time to assess their mindset, connect with their values, and bring empathy, active listening, and clear communication to the engagement. They show trust and honesty. They are enthusiastic while remaining present and demonstrate a willingness to participate, grow, learn, and achieve their definition of success through collaboration with a consultant.

WHAT IS HOLISTIC WILLINGNESS?

Genuine: Genuine willingness involves an active, engaged, and open attitude toward collaboration. It goes beyond merely agreeing to work with a consultant; it requires the client to show a deep commitment to the change process, listen to expert advice, and incorporate consultant feedback into decision-making. This kind of willingness demands a long-term perspective, where the client and consultant share a common goal of driving sustainable and impactful transformation. Key elements of genuine willingness include:

1. Openness to New Ideas: Clients should be open to considering perspectives that challenge their existing assumptions and operational paradigms.

2. Commitment to Change: A readiness to act on recommendations and implement changes demonstrates a willingness to make changes.

3. Mutual Respect and Trust: Genuine willingness creates a trusting environment where both parties appreciate each other's expertise.

4. Active Engagement: Clients regularly adhere to the recommendations and communicate openly.

Strong Example of Holistic Willingness

Consider a multinational company seeking assistance with employee engagement and morale. The client has attempted internal solutions, but something requires attention. Therefore, the client enlists a consultant who specializes in transforming corporate culture.

In this case, genuine, holistic willingness is shown through several vital actions. First, the leadership team openly examines the company's current culture and challenges. They remain open to feedback from all levels within the organization, even when it involves confronting uncomfortable truths about their management style and internal communications. The client fully invests in the diagnostic phase of the engagement, allowing consultants to engage with employees across departments and organizational levels. This openness facilitates a comprehensive understanding of the situation.

As the consultants suggest a new, inclusive approach to leadership development and team building, the client listens to the ideas and commits to piloting and implementing the proposed changes. They set up new feedback systems and encourage employees to participate in training programs, showing a willingness to integrate these changes into daily operations.

Leadership promotes transparency by holding themselves accountable for the change and fostering a culture of continuous improvement.

The client stays actively engaged throughout the process, offering continuous feedback, modifying strategies as needed, and consistently aligning their actions with the consultant's advice.

This approach reflects a sincere, comprehensive willingness to collaborate—embracing change, committing to action, and fostering a shared vision of transformation.

Weak Example of Holistic Willingness

Consider a different scenario: a company dealing with operational inefficiencies hires a consultant to optimize its processes. However, the willingness to work with the consultant is considerably more limited.

Initially, the leadership team seeks quick, superficial solutions. They bring in the consultant but aren't truly open to challenging the status quo.

They agree with the consultant's recommendations at a high level but make minimal changes to existing processes. They hesitate to question long-standing practices or the company's ingrained habits. The leadership team expresses support when the consultant suggests implementing new tools and restructuring workflows but lacks commitment to the necessary investments, whether in time, resources, or personnel.

Although the consultant's expertise is superficially acknowledged, genuine engagement never occurs. The consultant's feedback is not fully implemented, and there is no significant follow-up or effort to track progress. When challenges arise, the leadership team often falls back on old methods instead of working through the change process, indicating a reluctance to navigate the complexities of transformation.

This weak example of willingness illustrates a passive agreement to work with a consultant without fully committing to the essential actions needed for lasting change. The client must prioritize the relationship or the suggested strategies, leading to a disengaged, ineffective partnership.

KEY POINTS ON WILLINGNESS

1. Openness to New Ideas: A client demonstrates willingness by listening to and considering new ways of thinking and operating, even if they challenge the status quo.

2. Commitment to Action: A genuinely willing client doesn't merely accept advice; they take concrete steps to implement it and adapt their practices as needed.

3. Trust and Respect: Genuine willingness requires fostering a culture of mutual respect in which both the consultant and client feel appreciated. Trust develops gradually through ongoing communication, openness, and reliability.

4. Active Engagement: A truly willing client stays engaged in the process, providing ongoing feedback, adjusting strategies as necessary, and assuming responsibility for the change effort.

When genuinely embraced, willingness becomes a powerful force that can greatly enhance the outcomes of a consulting engagement. The strongest consulting relationships are founded on mutual respect, active collaboration, and a shared commitment to transformation. In contrast, weak or half-hearted willingness often leads to missed opportunities for growth, stalled initiatives, and reduced value from the consultant's expertise.

Understanding the extent of a client's willingness is vital for customizing engagement strategies and establishing realistic expectations. For clients, nurturing a culture of authentic willingness within the organization can lead to more meaningful, impactful, and sustainable change. Ultimately, authentic willingness sparks success in any consulting partnership, allowing both parties to align their goals, invest in the process, and achieve lasting results.

CONCLUSION

As you close this book, your journey to becoming an exceptional consulting client comes full circle.

By now, you've explored the nuances of consulting relationships, strategies for optimal outcomes, and establishing the mindset required for collaborative success. This final chapter synthesizes key insights, actionable takeaways, and a vision for nurturing partnerships that drive transformative results.

At its core, consulting is a partnership. Consultants provide expertise, frameworks, and objectivity, while clients offer organizational context, resources, and decision-making authority. Exceptional clients understand that their role is not merely to "hire and wait" but to co-create solutions alongside their consultants. Viewing consulting as a transaction— where the consultant delivers a pre-packaged solution—restricts your value. Instead, approach it as a collaborative endeavor. Be ready to engage in dialogue, share information openly, and challenge assumptions constructively.

Clients and consultants possess complementary expertise. While consultants bring specialized knowledge and fresh perspectives, clients offer deep organizational insights. Acknowledging and leveraging this combined expertise enhances the partnership. Significant engagements begin with clarity. Before engaging consultants, ask yourself: What specific outcomes are you after? What problem are you solving, or what opportunity are you pursuing? Establish a shared understanding of success. This involves setting clear goals, establishing timelines, and defining metrics to assess progress. For instance, rather than stating, "We want to improve our marketing strategy," clarify by saying, "We aim to increase lead conversion by 20% within six months."

Clarity regarding scope and resources is just as important. Ensure the consultant knows the budget, time limitations, and organizational dynamics they must navigate. Establishing these boundaries from the outset helps avoid misalignment and scope creep.

Communication is the lifeblood of any consulting relationship. The more openly and frequently you communicate, the more likely the engagement will yield positive results. Be candid about your organization's challenges and dynamics.

Consultants rely on accurate information to diagnose issues and create solutions. Avoid withholding critical details for fear of appearing vulnerable; trust is built through transparency. Schedule regular check-ins to assess progress, address obstacles, and provide feedback. A weekly or bi-weekly update can help ensure the project remains on track and that any necessary course corrections occur promptly.

Empowering Consultants to Deliver

Once consultants are engaged, they require your support to perform their roles effectively. This includes providing them access to the resources, people, and information necessary to deliver results. Excellent clients assist consultants in navigating internal networks. This may involve introducing them to key stakeholders or facilitating discussions with frontline employees who possess valuable insights.

Consultants must often challenge the status quo or bring uncomfortable truths to light.

Create an environment that encourages them to speak candidly without fear of repercussions. This openness typically leads to the most transformative insights.

Influential clients maintain a balance between being engaged and allowing consultants the autonomy to carry out their tasks. Trust the expertise you've hired. Micromanaging consultants waste your time and diminish your ability to think creatively and independently. While you shouldn't micromanage, it's crucial to stay informed. Conduct regular check-ins to ask questions, provide feedback, and ensure alignment without dictating every detail.

Consulting engagements often challenge existing mindsets, processes, or structures. Excellent clients tackle these challenges with curiosity and a readiness to adapt. It's natural to want to protect your organization's current practices, but being defensive can hinder progress. Instead, see feedback and recommendations as opportunities for growth, even if they feel uncomfortable.

Recommendations often require an internal champion to gain traction. Be ready to advocate for the consultant's insights and suggestions within your organization, particularly among skeptical stakeholders.

Feedback is a two-way street. As consultants provide feedback on your organization, you should also give feedback on their work.

If you have concerns about the consultant's approach or deliverables, address them promptly. Instead of giving vague critiques, offer specific examples of what could be improved. Positive reinforcement is essential as well. Recognizing good work boosts morale and reinforces the behaviors and practices you want to continue.

Committing to Follow-Through

One of the most frustrating outcomes of a consulting engagement is when recommendations go unused. Great clients ensure that insights and solutions are implemented effectively. Consultants often leave organizations with new tools, frameworks, or processes. Invest in training and resources to ensure your team can maintain these changes after the engagement ends. Don't just assess the engagement at its conclusion. Monitor how the consultant's recommendations affect your organization over time and use these insights to guide future engagements.

The best consulting clients view engagements as opportunities for learning and growth, not just for problem-solving. Great clients treat consulting projects as chances to enhance their organization's learning capacity. They document lessons learned, celebrate successes, and analyze missteps to strengthen future initiatives. Working with consultants can also help you develop as a leader. Actively engage in the process, seek feedback on your role, and reflect on improving your leadership practices.

The most successful consulting engagements often result in lasting relationships. Viewing your consultants as long-term partners instead of short-term problem-solvers can unlock tremendous value. Building trust takes time, but the rewards are significant in the long run. When consultants feel trusted and valued, they are more likely to exceed expectations in supporting your organization's success. Consultants who deeply understand your organization can provide quicker, more customized solutions in future engagements. You can foster continuity by collaborating with consultants who understand your goals, challenges, and culture.

The Consulting Relationship: A Two-Way Street

The foundation of any successful consulting engagement lies in recognizing that it is not a one-sided transaction but a collaborative relationship. Great clients invest as much in the process as their consultants do. They share their vision openly, provide timely feedback, and remain committed to the shared objectives. This reciprocal dynamic forms the bedrock of trust and mutual respect.

Like any endeavor, preparation significantly influences the outcome. Before hiring a consultant, clarify your objectives, prioritize your needs, and ensure internal stakeholders are aligned. A well-prepared client sets the stage for consultants to deliver their best work.

The consulting relationship is often perceived as one-sided: the consultant offers expertise, while the client enjoys the benefits. Though this simplified perspective emphasizes the value of consultants, it overlooks an important truth: effective consulting is inherently reciprocal. A two-way relationship founded on mutual respect, open communication, and shared accountability is crucial for achieving transformative results.

Examining the dynamics of the consulting relationship begins with emphasizing both parties' responsibilities, expectations, and contributions. Analyzing key aspects of collaboration—including trust-building, co-creation, adaptability, and feedback loops—offers insights into how consultants and clients can develop partnerships that create maximum value for both sides.

A successful consulting relationship begins with trust. With trust, even the most skilled consultant can secure buy-in or drive meaningful change. Trust is established through transparency, authenticity, and consistency from both parties.

This entails expertise without arrogance, offering evidence-based recommendations, and honestly acknowledging their limitations. For clients, trust requires openness about challenges, a willingness to share critical data, and confidence in the consultant's dedication to their success.

Aligning goals and expectations is equally important. Misaligned expectations can derail a project early, as both parties may pursue divergent visions of success.

In the initial stages, consultants and clients should collaborate to define objectives, key performance indicators (KPIs), and timelines. This collaboration fosters a sense of shared ownership and ensures that both sides work toward a common purpose.

Contrary to the myth that "outsiders fix everything," clients play a crucial role in consulting. While consultants offer expertise and frameworks, the implementation—and ultimately the success—hinges on the client's involvement. Consultants bring valuable external knowledge, but clients are the true experts within their organizations. They deeply understand internal culture, power dynamics, and historical context. By sharing this insight, clients empower consultants to customize their recommendations, ensuring greater relevance and practicality.

Organizations require internal advocates for recommendations to take hold. Clients should identify and empower individuals who champion change, convey its significance, and exemplify desired behaviors. This internal support often dictates whether a consultant's insights translate into action or remain theoretical.

Consulting often reveals uncomfortable truths, such as inefficiencies, entrenched practices that deserve challenge, or unfamiliar approaches that may need to be proposed. Clients should be ready to embrace this discomfort, viewing it as a chance for growth instead of threatening the status quo.

The Consultant's Role: Facilitator, Not Fixer

While consultants are hired for their expertise, their primary role is facilitating transformation rather than imposing solutions. The most impactful consultants view themselves as enablers, guiding clients to discover, own, and implement solutions. Effective consulting starts with deep listening. Consultants must resist the urge to jump to conclusions or recycle old solutions. Instead, they should immerse themselves in the client's context to fully understand their unique challenges and aspirations. Cookie-cutter approaches rarely yield lasting results. The best consultants adapt their frameworks, tools, and methodologies to suit clients' needs. This customization enhances relevance and demonstrates respect for the client's unique circumstances.

While clients expect consultants to offer fresh perspectives, an overly directive approach can alienate crucial stakeholders. Consultants must balance confidently sharing insights with remaining open to client input. This humility fosters collaboration and ensures that solutions are co-created rather than imposed. A hallmark of a two-way consulting relationship is co-creation. When consultants and clients work together on solutions, they leverage the strengths of both parties, leading to more effective and sustainable outcomes.

Co-creation involves more than just the consultant and the executive sponsor; it requires input from various stakeholders.

This inclusivity ensures solutions address the perspectives and needs of those most affected. When clients actively contribute to developing strategies, they gain a sense of ownership. This emotional investment enhances the likelihood of follow-through and diminishes resistance to change. Co-creation thrives on iteration. Instead of presenting a polished, final solution, consultants and clients work together to refine ideas, test hypotheses, and adapt based on feedback. This iterative process guarantees that solutions are both innovative and practical. Even the most collaborative consulting relationships encounter challenges. Acknowledging and addressing these obstacles is vital to sustaining a productive partnership.

Miscommunication regarding scope, deliverables, or timelines can strain the relationship. Regular check-ins and a willingness to recalibrate ensure both parties remain aligned. Change is inherently disruptive, and resistance is natural. Consultants can address this by identifying potential barriers early and collaborating with clients to develop strategies for overcoming them. Clients, lacking input from consultants, hold the ultimate decision-making authority, which can sometimes lead to premature dismissals. Conversely, consultants may need to advocate for their agenda more forcefully. A spirit of mutual respect and shared purpose fosters balance in these dynamics.

Feedback Loops: A Continuous Process

Feedback is essential in a two-way consulting relationship. It allows both parties to learn, adapt, and enhance their collaboration. Right from the beginning, consultants and clients should agree on feedback mechanisms for giving and receiving input. This could include regular debriefs, surveys, or casual check-ins. Feedback should be honest yet constructive. Both parties must approach it with a growth mindset, viewing it as a chance to improve rather than a reason for blame.

While feedback often emphasizes improvement areas, recognizing successes is just as crucial.

Celebrating wins strengthens relationships and reinforces positive behaviors. The most effective consulting relationships extend beyond the duration of a single project. They evolve into long-term partnerships defined by ongoing collaboration and mutual growth. Over time, consultants acquire a deep understanding of the client's organization, enabling them to offer more nuanced and strategic advice. Likewise, clients become more skilled at leveraging the consultant's expertise.

In lasting partnerships, both parties serve as learners and teachers. Consultants share emerging best practices, while clients offer real-world insights that enhance the consultant's methodologies. Long-term relationships emphasize immediate results and bolster the client's capacity for sustained success. This may involve developing internal leaders, increasing organizational agility, or fostering a culture of continuous improvement.

One frequently overlooked aspect of being a great client is what happens after the consultant departs. The most effective clients ensure that insights are implemented and institutionalized, allowing the organization to reap benefits long after the engagement concludes.

A Final Word

Being a great consulting client is as much an art as consulting itself. It requires a proactive mindset, a willingness to collaborate, and a commitment to mutual success.

By recognizing the importance of partnership, establishing objectives, communicating effectively, and promoting change, you can ensure your consulting engagements address immediate issues and create lasting value for your organization.

Great consulting relationships develop over time and require mutual effort. When both clients and consultants give their best, the results can be transformative for the organization and everyone involved in the journey.

Becoming an excellent consulting client is both an art and a science. It demands self-awareness, humility, and a dedication to growth.

By embodying the principles in this book, you will be well-positioned for project success and foster relationships that inspire innovation, build capacity, and unlock new possibilities for your organization.

As you embark on your next consulting engagement, remember that the best clients aren't just recipients of expertise but active co-creators of value. By embracing this role with confidence and intention, you can transform your organization's outcomes and the consulting industry.

ABOUT THE AUTHORS

DR. CURTIS ODOM is an Associate Professor of Management and Organizational Development at the D'Amore-McKim School of Business at Northeastern University, a Senior Member of the Forbes Coaches Council, and a Harvard Business Review Advisory Council member. Curtis is also a management consultant, best-selling author, ICF professional certified coach, and former Fortune 50 executive who consults and coaches from his experience of getting results.

Additionally, Curtis is the Managing Partner at Prescient Strategists, a Boston-based management consulting firm serving Fortune 100 companies, colleges, and universities. The award-winning firm delivers change management, strategic workforce planning, executive leadership coaching, and leadership development solutions to clients during mergers and acquisitions and other large-scale business transformation initiatives. Curtis is often called on to be a trusted advisor during the seismic shifts organizations must make to accelerate change and strategic growth within their workforce beyond evolutionary advancements. Clients trust his team as trusted advisors on targeted business transformations to enable their organizations to compete more effectively while making strategic human capital pivots.

Curtis earned a Doctor of Education with honors from Pepperdine University. He also completed Executive Education programs at the Wharton School at the University of Pennsylvania, the MIT Sloan School of Management, and Cornell University. Before his industry and academic careers, Curtis served on active duty for ten years in the United States Navy, including combat deployment during Operation Desert Storm.

SOPHIA BARRETT is a project manager working in the Greater Boston area. She received a BA from Skidmore College with a major in Anthropology and an MBA from the D'Amore McKim School of Business at Northeastern University with concentrations in Organizational Leadership and Healthcare Management.

Sophia's areas of expertise lie in knowledge management, strategic measurement, and process improvement, with experience working in healthcare, startup, non-profit, and higher education environments.

When not working, Sophia plays heavy metal drums, sings opera (although not simultaneously), and composes elaborate tabletop role-playing games full of adventure. Sophia currently lives in the Boston area with their partner and their dog.